PARENTING · with · SPIRITUAL POWER

Julie K. Nelson

CFI

AN IMPRINT OF CEDAR FORT, INC.
SPRINGVILLE, UTAH

ISBN 13: 978-1-4621-1168-8

Published by CFI an imprint of Cedar Fort, Inc., 2373 W. 700 S., Springville, UT 84663
Distributed by Cedar Fort, Inc., www.cedarfort.com

LIBRARY OF CONGRESS CATALOGING-IN-PUBLICATION DATA

Nelson, Julie K., 1963- author.
Parenting with spiritual power / Julie K. Nelson.
     pages cm
  ISBN 978-1-4621-1168-8
  1. Parenting--Religious aspects--Church of Jesus Christ of Latter-day Saints. 2. Parents in the Bible. 3. Parents in the Book of Mormon. 4. Church of Jesus Christ of Latter-day Saints--Doctrines. I. Title.
  BS579.H8N45 2013
  248.8'45--dc23

                    2012048492

Cover design by Rebecca J. Greenwood
Cover design © 2013 by Lyle Mortimer
Edited and typeset by Whitney A. Lindsley

Printed in the United States of America

10 9 8 7 6 5 4 3 2 1

 *Praise for*

PARENTING WITH
SPIRITUAL POWER

"We have always thought that the best way to study the scriptures was to think of the people we are reading about as friends. Julie Nelson has captured that and more as she challenges us to think of some of our heroes in the scriptures as inspiring parents. Her ability to bring it down to the things that parents are facing daily is brilliant. This book is extraordinary as it examines what these scriptural friends taught their children by word and deed. Julie transforms scripture stories into advice we can use as we deal with parenting issues that appear so frequently in our own parenting experience."

Richard and Linda Eyre, #1 *New York Times* best-selling authors
of *Teaching Your Children Values*

"We don't often think of scripture as a source of parenting principles. That is about to change for you as you read this book. You will be inspired to be a better parent regardless of the ages of your children or the challenges they present. Nuggets and kernels of parenting help explodes from these pages from scriptural events familiar to Latter-day Saints and sustained by the teachings of living prophets. Written in an engaging style with powerful examples and illustrations, this writing will remind parents of the power of gospel principles to assist them in their sacred stewardship of rearing the children of our Father in Heaven."

Douglas E. Brinley, coauthor of *Then Comes Marriage* and
Between Husband and Wife: Gospel Perspectives on Marital Intimacy

"Julie Nelson has done it! She has produced an easy-to-apply parenting manual based on the scriptures! This book helps us learn from parents in the scriptures who also faced the challenge of raising righteous children in a wicked world. This book is filled with real-life examples as well—moving stories from parents today. Julie's discussion questions not only give parents principles and ideas to talk about but also some concrete ideas for improving parent-child relationships. And who doesn't need help in that department?"

Brad Wilcox, author of *The Continuous Atonement*

"I was delighted to find this new parenting book by Julie Nelson, full of inspiring stories and scriptural ties. This is a great book for parents of any age to help us reexamine our parenting habits and then improve upon them through applying gospel principles. It will join my short list of favorite parenting books!"

Sean Covey, best-selling author of *The 7 Habits of Highly Effective Teens* and
The 6 Most Important Decisions You'll Ever Make

"Sometimes we forget that the stories of the scriptures have been preserved to teach us how to live the doctrines that are contained therein. Sister Nelson reminds us that our beloved scriptural characters were parents and children, like us. She tells us that "whatever we have or are now experiencing as parents, we can find a mother or father within the standard works that has walked a similar path." By compiling these great parenting methods into one book, she gives us practical solutions to help our children along the path to the Savior and provides us with specific questions to help us ponder our next step. This is a great resource for anyone striving to raise righteous children in a wicked world."

Fran C. Hafen, author of *Joy Cometh in the Morning:*
A Story of Healing from the Loss of a Child

 **This book is dedicated to**

*My parents who have always loved me and my children
and taught me to love the scriptures.*

*My children: Heavenly Father must truly love me to
have given you to me.*

*My husband: You are my true center of
unfailing support and love.*

Acknowledgments

I am deeply indebted to those who read through earlier manuscript versions and made significant suggestions and corrections. This book would not be as it is without their selfless contributions. Thank you!

I also express my most profound gratitude for those who have shared their personal parenting experiences with me over the years and graciously allowed me to use them. Your stories pulse life into every page.

And I give special thanks to the creative team at Cedar Fort, Inc., who welcomed and encouraged me and turned my words into something beautiful.

 # Contents

CONTENTS

*His word was in mine heart as a burning fire shut up
in my bones . . . and I could not stay.*

Jeremiah 20:9

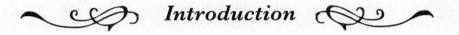 **Introduction**

I wish children came with an instruction manual! How many times have
we heard this lament by a frustrated or overwhelmed parent? Perhaps
we have said these words (or thought them) ourselves. There are "how
to" manuals for practically anything: installing a new faucet, building a
remote control car, baking an apple pie, refinishing an antique chair, or
assembling a bicycle. Is there a formula or a perfect manual for raising
children? In our quest for seeking answers, Elder Kevin R. Duncan of the
Seventy warned,

> This world is full of so many self-help books, so many self-proclaimed
> experts, so many theorists, educators, and philosophers who have
> advice and counsel to give on any and all subjects. With technology
> today, information on a myriad of subjects is available with the click of
> a keystroke. It is easy to get caught in the trap of looking to the "arm
> of flesh" for advice on everything from how to raise children to how to
> find happiness. While some information has merit, as members of the
> Church we have access to the source of pure truth, even God Himself.
> We would do well to search out answers to our problems and questions
> by investigating what the Lord has revealed through His prophets.
> With that same technology today, we have at our fingertips access to
> the words of the prophets on nearly any subject.[1]

1

Our loving Father in Heaven has given us *the* manual for parenthood—the holy scriptures together with the inspired words of our modern prophets, seers, and revelators. This is the road map to follow as we pray for safety and direction in life. President Boyd K. Packer said, "There is in the scriptures . . . counsel, commandments, even warnings that we are to protect, to love, to care for, and to 'teach [children] to walk in the ways of truth [Mosiah 4:15].'"[2] Elder Russell M. Nelson observed, "[Our Creator] did not leave us alone. He provided a guide—a spiritual road map—to help us achieve success in our journey. We call that guide the standard works. . . . As you ponder and pray about doctrinal principles, the Holy Ghost will speak to your mind and your heart [D&C 8:2]. *From events portrayed in the scriptures, new insights will come and principles relevant to your situation will distill upon your heart.*"[3] Indeed, parents navigating today's world are more likely to achieve success when their practices are based on revealed truth and are guided by the Holy Ghost.

Parents who consistently and prayerfully read the standard works with an open heart and mind allow the Holy Ghost to reveal how to apply the truths therein. Nephi did "liken all scriptures unto us, that it might be for our profit and learning" (1 Nephi 19:23). Elder Boyd K. Packer testified to the truth of Nephi's words: "I took that to mean that the scriptures are likened to me personally, and that is true of everyone else."[4]

The prophet Moroni gave us the formula for finding truth and promises us power in parenting. Before burying the plates, he exhorted us to read the words written thereon. Assuredly, if we pray with a "sincere heart, with real intent, having faith in Christ, [God] will manifest the truth of it unto you, by the power of the Holy Ghost" (Moroni 10:5). He further expanded his promise to seekers of all truth, including those trying to embrace successful parenting practices. "And by the power of the Holy Ghost ye may know the truth of *all* things" (Moroni 10:6; emphasis added). Parents must read the words of the prophets and apostles under the direction of the Spirit and apply principles to meet their child's individual needs.

Prophets such as Adam and other prominent figures in the scriptures offer myriad examples of righteous people who did their best at parenting. Whatever we have experienced or are now experiencing as parents, we can find a mother or father within the standard works that has walked a similar path. We rejoice over parents who raised righteous children and mourn when even their best efforts turned into discouragement and anguish. We can be encouraged too that good people from the scriptures, like us, were not perfect parents.

Prophets were not exempt from severe disappointments in child rearing. Adam's son Cain murdered his sibling (see Moses 5:32–33), and Lehi's two eldest sons attempted to murder their father (see 1 Nephi 2:13). Mosiah and Alma struggled for years with rebellious sons who "went about destroying the church" and causing "a great hinderment to the prosperity of the church" (Mosiah 27:8–9). Eli had two sons who were also temple priests. They took sacrificial meat from the altar for their own use, committed adultery, and caused the people to commit sin by their example (see 1 Samuel 2:22–24). Zeniff in the Book of Mormon knew a little about substance abuse. His son, King Noah, entertained himself with concubines and was described as a "wine bibber," or an alcoholic (see Mosiah 11:14–15). Even Alma the Younger's son engaged in immorality during his mission and left the ministry (see Alma 39).

Parents today struggle with these same issues, as well as many others, leaving us searching for answers. Truly we are raising our children behind enemy lines. The world is embattled between forces of light and dark, between truth and error. What worked in the past is not enough in our latter days. "For we wrestle not against flesh and blood, but against principalities, against powers, against the rulers of the darkness of this world, against spiritual wickedness in high *places*. Wherefore take unto you the whole armour of God, that ye may be able to withstand in the evil day, and having done all, to stand" (Ephesians 6:12–13; emphasis added). We arm ourselves by knowing and living the word of God, by hearkening to the counsel of our modern-day prophets and apostles and following the Spirit that whispers truth and peace to each parent who seeks understanding.

The scriptures show us that even the best parenting practices do not guarantee righteous children. Agency is given to all people, including those who would abuse it. Nevertheless, a righteous parent's conduct is a case study in what to do when children turn away from correct teachings. We can learn from scriptural examples of perseverance in parenting, hope in the eternal plan of happiness, and firm faith in the process of repentance and in the power of divine love. The estimable lessons about parenting in difficult circumstances are as important to study and learn from as those of successfully raised children.

By the same token, the scriptures are replete with examples of worthy parents who were not blessed with goodly parents themselves. They are a testament to free will and the power to change. We are not destined to repeat the same mistakes as our own parents. We should not perpetuate the unrighteous dominion modeled in our past. Abraham was raised by a father who was idolatrous and offered him up as a sacrifice (see Abraham 1:5–7), but he left his father's wicked country and influence and started anew. This is a message for us to leave poor habits and attitudes about parenting behind. Abraham overcame his circumstances and became an honorable parent and the father of Isaac and Ishmael. His name means "father of a multitude."

The following chapters highlight noteworthy people from the scriptures who walked the earth. These parents' and leaders' experiences are preserved for us today—to inspire us, to teach us, to cause us to reflect on ways we can improve. What would they tell us if we could ask them how to be better parents? Through their examples, Alma the Younger showed us how to chastise a child with love; Lehi taught us how to nurture ourselves spiritually and never give up on wayward children; Jacob reminded us that forgiveness is necessary for healing within a family of strife.

Each scriptural parent has an abundance of wisdom to share with us by the way he or she lived. To examine these timeless truths is the purpose of this book. You will read of powerful parenting examples and suggestions for personal application. These will allow you to ponder and act on ways to build a better parenting partnership with your Heavenly Father. There are discussion questions after the last chapter to help guide you in making positive changes in your parenting practices, which can bring a greater Spirit into your home, confidence and peace into your hearts, and love into your family relationships.

Each chapter presents selected scriptural events and general principles. We all need to pray for and seek after the gift of discernment for specific application. In addition to the several studies presented here, we can "liken" other scriptural passages in our personal search for answers. "We all *need* guidance through life," explained Elder Russell M. Nelson. "We *obtain* it best from the standard works and teachings of the prophets of God. With diligent effort, we can *achieve* that guidance and thus qualify for all of the blessings that God has in store for His faithful children."[5] To that end, we can be assured that "all [our] children shall be taught of the Lord; and great shall be the peace of [our] children" (Isaiah 54:13).

NOTES

1. Kevin R. Duncan, "Our Very Survival," *Ensign*, November 2010, 35.

2. Boyd K. Packer, "Children," *Ensign*, May 2002, 8.

3. Russell M. Nelson, "Living by Scriptural Guidance," *Ensign*, November 2000, 17–18.

4. Boyd K. Packer, "The Book of Mormon: Another Testament of Jesus Christ," *Ensign*, May 2005, 7.

5. Russell M. Nelson, "Living by Scriptural Guidance," *Ensign*, November 2000, 18.

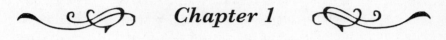

Chapter 1

GOD AND ADAM AND EVE: THE POWER OF AGENCY

Our first parents were in the presence of their Heavenly Parent in the Garden of Eden. They walked and talked with God every day. God is the perfection in parenting. Therefore, we can learn much about righteous principles in raising children from the account in Genesis and Pearl of Great Price and the interaction between God and Adam and Eve.

The overarching principle we learn from the plan of salvation, authored by our Father in Heaven, is agency. "And I, the Lord God, commanded the man, saying: Of every tree of the garden thou mayest eat, but of the tree of knowledge of good and evil, thou shalt not eat of it, nevertheless, thou mayest choose for thyself, for it is given unto thee" (Moses 3:16–17). In other words, God allowed Adam and Eve a freedom of choices within set boundaries to encourage them to exercise their agency responsibly.

In this primordial account, we might become preoccupied with the single "don't" and its associated restriction and forget all the "do's." God offered his children *every* tree and plant to eat from, excepting one. Adam and Eve could choose from an abundance of God's creations to enjoy within boundaries. The same environment should be created and exercised in our homes. Not only should we express far more positive statements than negative (at least an 8:1 ratio), but options should also be offered in a positive manner. For example, if a child asks if he can play with a friend, but has a few chores to do first, we can consider contrasting approaches. Agency without boundaries would allow the child to play regardless of his chores. Agency within boundaries can be phrased in a negative or positive way. Our knee-jerk reaction could be, "No you can't. You've got a lot of chores to do first." How discouraging does that sound? Using the Garden of Eden account, we could reframe our approach to the positive with the "can" rather than the "can't." "Yes, you can play just as soon as your chores are done. It won't take long, and then you'll be off with your friend!" This is a more encouraging statement. If we build up a larger balance of positives as we guide and teach children, the few restrictive statements will seem less negative and the child will more likely be agreeable.

Agency and consequence are inseparable. God presented choices and their consequences to Adam and Eve, such as "Thou mayest choose for thyself . . . but, remember that I forbid it, for in the day thou eatest thereof thou shalt surely die" (Moses 3:17). His expectations were clearly outlined with consequences. If these rules were disobeyed, Adam and Eve knew in advance that they alone were responsible for the outcome. We should do likewise with our children. My nine-year-old son was having trouble cleaning his room one day, and he knew he couldn't play until it was done. I encouraged him along the way, but he was still dawdling. I finally made this observation in a friendly tone: "It will be so sad if your friend calls to play and you will have to tell him you aren't finished cleaning your room." My son smiled and said, "You got me there, Mom!" and picked up the pace. Here are some statements that clearly define consequences and expectations:

- "When you throw the blocks, they will need to be put away for a while so they don't hurt anyone."

- "I am only able to wash dirty laundry that is brought into the laundry room."

- "I will be able to talk with you as soon as your voice sounds calm like mine."

When God explained a consequence, Adam and Eve were certain of the outcome. Children also need to know the consequence is sure and their parent will not waiver. Consider the previous scenarios. How would the child feel if she continued throwing blocks, but the parent did not put them away? How resolutely would a child pick up his dirty laundry if he knew his mother would wash it anyway? Similarly, what if the child continued yelling, but the parent raised her voice in return? We should be as accountable to our children as they are to us. Therefore, we should avoid creating consequences we are unable or unwilling to uphold. Making empty threats is contrary to our Father's plan. Our stewardship over family is about creating safe boundaries, and it is compromised when we cannot be trusted in our word and deed.

When presenting options, we also need to put them in a context of what is acceptable and what is not. "I'm not okay with your riding in the street yet. Please keep your bike on the sidewalk." Notice that the parent gives the child what *to do* rather than just what *not* to do. We can also solicit our child's help in creating options so he can exercise his agency and be part of the problem-solving process. Ask the child what solutions are possible and then discuss what would work for you both. For example, a child might have a weekly job to mow the lawn but argues he cannot do it one week due to lack of time. As you sympathize, you can state that it is not acceptable to completely abdicate their family contribution. What *is* acceptable, however, is finding some other way to contribute. Perhaps the child chooses a manageable chore instead you both agree on. Or perhaps the child offers to do an extra chore when they return to mowing the lawn the following week. Essential to this problem-solving process is the parent valuing the child's ideas and concerns.

Whenever possible, like God's example in the Garden of Eden, there should be more acceptable choices than undesirable ones. With a two-year-old, I find it much easier to ask, "Would you like to wear the red coat or your brown sweater?" or "Pick which coat you'd like to wear" than demanding, "Get your coat on." (Tantrum ensues.) "No, you *have* to wear a coat! You can't go outside in your T-shirt." When we shower our children with encouraging and positive statements, we present more appealing possibilities that outweigh the bad choices they could make. We give them many opportunities to experience and feel the effects of righteous living and using sound judgment.

After Adam and Eve chose to eat the fruit, they reacted in a way we typically see in guilty children. They ran to hide. In Moses 4:15, God called them out, saying, "Where goest thou?" I am certain God knew exactly where they were but gave them the opportunity to come forward and be accountable for their own choices. A large measure of maturation takes place each time we allow children to speak for their actions and motives. God listened to Adam's confession and followed with another question: "Who told thee thou wast naked? Hast thou eaten of the tree whereof I commanded thee that thou shouldst not eat, if so thou shouldst surely die?" (Moses 4:17). Again, God knew what had taken place. All things are present before His omnipresent eye. He repeated the perfect pattern of parenting: gather information and allow children to answer for themselves. In each case, he asked and then listened.

The interaction between God and Adam and Eve presents a parent being centered on the development of the child and the parent-child relationship. Listening is such a critical piece in this process. We live in a world that worships technology and seeks after endless entertainment. Glamorous figures, enticing pleasures, and even day-to-day demands often overshadow a reluctant, discouraged child. We need to stop, listen, and validate when strong emotions are expressed. Validation is more than just listening; we show our children their ideas and feelings matter. Here is an example between a child and parent:

"I don't want to go to school today. I wish we had never moved!"

"It was hard to move away from your old school, wasn't it?"

"Why did you have to get a new job? Why couldn't we just stay where we were?"

"You liked your old friends. I know how happy you were there."

"Yes, I was. I don't have any friends now. The kids just ignore me and I have no one to sit next to at lunch."

"Wow. That sounds hard! What do you do at lunchtime?"

"I just sit there by myself." (Child begins to cry and parent holds her close.)

Parent and child embrace for a while until the child stops crying.

"I can't imagine how lonely you must feel. I love you so much and you have been so brave with this move. (Pause.) What do you want to do about school today?"

Long pause.

"I guess I'll go. The bus is going to be here soon."

"Is there anything you can do to make the lunch situation better?"

"I'll think about it. Maybe there's someone who is by herself that I can sit with."

"It's hard right now but I know things will get better. If you want, you can tell me how lunch went when you get home today. Bye. I love you."

Here is a contrasting example of the same scenario:

"I don't want to go to school today. I wish we had never moved!"

"You have to go. That's life. I'm leaving for work soon, and you can't stay here by yourself!"

"Why did you have to get a new job? Why couldn't we just stay where we were?"

"We've been over this a hundred times. You'll just have to get over it and start making friends here."

"But I don't have any friends! That's the whole point! They all hate me and so do you!

"I don't hate you. You are overreacting."

"No I'm not! And I'm never going back to school again!" (Child runs into his room and slams the door shut).

The parent in the first example gained trust by validating the child's initial emotion (not wanting to go to school and yearning for her old life). In that proximity of trust, the child was able to articulate her deepest pain: sitting alone at lunch. In the second example, the parent shut down the child and was never able to discover the loneliness at lunch. The first parent did not rush to fix the problem but just listened empathetically. He expressed love and concern and allowed the child to work through her emotional inner struggle. By the end, the child knew the parent was aware of her fears and that her feelings were important. That engendered confidence in the child's ability to express herself and move forward.

Jesus listened and validated with perfect charity during his ministry. When he walked down a crowded street one day, he and his disciples were pressed on all sides. Yet he knew when a woman reached out to touch the hem of his garment and felt virtue leave him to heal her. He asked first, "Who touched me?" to allow the woman the opportunity to come forward. This is similar to the exchange in the Garden of Eden. Next, he *turned* and looked around to find her. Trembling, the woman fell at his feet and confessed what she had done. He listened and did not discredit her feelings—an important part of validation. He assuaged her fears by tenderly calling her "daughter" and offering peace. He listened to her face to face—acknowledging her worth. "Daughter, thy faith hath made thee whole; go in peace, and be whole of thy plague" (Mark 5:34). Jesus did not have to stop; she was healed regardless. Nevertheless, he validated the power of her personal faith. The exchange—personal in this crowded, public place—tells the importance of strengthening others and allowing them to express their fears and desires.

My mother-in-law shared a poignant story about turning and listening. Her husband was in the military, which left her with the majority of the task of caring for the needs of their nine children. She was industrious and often found herself at the sewing machine, making her children's clothing. One of her teenage daughters began talking to her about something important, and my mother-in-law listened over the hum of the machine with her back facing her daughter. Her daughter became more frustrated as she attempted to engage her mother. She said, "Listen to me, Mom." Her mother replied, "I *am* listening, honey, and I'm sewing a dress for *you*," and continued working. She finally took her mother's hands off the sewing table and grasped them in her two hands. She spun her mother around and looked directly in her eyes. "No, *listen* to me, Mom!" Not always will our children be as forceful in communicating their needs. Especially adolescents. Our Heavenly Father is never too busy to listen. His back is never turned.

President Ezra Taft Benson recalled sweet memories of his mother's teaching in their meager farmhouse. Note how his mother, laden with work, recognized a teaching moment and an impressionable young child:

> I can still see her in my mind's eye bending over the ironing board with newspapers on the floor, ironing long strips of white cloth, with beads of perspiration on her forehead. When I asked her what she was doing, she said, "These are temple robes, my son. Your father and I are going to the temple at Logan."
>
> Then she put the old flatiron on the stove, drew a chair close to mine, and told me about temple work—how important it is to be able to go to the temple and participate in the sacred ordinances performed there. She also expressed her fervent hope that someday her children and grandchildren and great-grandchildren would have the opportunity to enjoy these priceless blessings.[1]

From the reign of Nephi until King Mosiah, families were subjected to the will of the king—good or evil. If the king was good, he persuaded righteous conduct. On the contrary, a tyrant caused his people to stumble in sin. This system of governance was inequitable; it gave too much power and responsibility to the king for the choices of his people. Their sins were answered upon his head (see Mosiah 29:31). It also deprived the people of their liberties and an "equal chance throughout the land" for every man

(Mosiah 29:38). In Mosiah chapter 29, King Mosiah laid out the case for no more kings to rule over them but that each man be accountable for himself. He articulated "that these things ought not to be; but that the burden should come upon all the people, that every man might bear his part" (Mosiah 29:34). Mosiah appealed to their reason that they be judged by judges and the natural tendencies for men to do good.

Too many parents govern their families counter to Mosiah's pattern of parenting. We should not rule with an iron fist but follow instead the supreme example of our Heavenly Father. Consider the following scenario and how the lessons learned in the Garden of Eden and Mosiah's kingdom can apply. Remember the principles of agency, offering appealing choices within limits ("every tree except this one"), asking, listening, self-governance, and validating the child's feelings. This parent has just found out her teenager wants to attend a party where there will be little or no adult supervision and the activities are suspect.

"Hi, Michael. What do you have going on tonight?"

"A party at Roger's house."

"I'd like to hear more about what adult will be responsible and what you'll be doing."

"I don't know. Maybe his parents will be there."

"It sounds a little uncertain. Why do you want to go so badly?"

"Because I was lucky enough to be invited and all the popular people will be there."

"Oh, I see. Those are some compelling reasons. Popularity *is* such a part of high school life. I love you, and I'm a little concerned about your safety. I'd like to see if there are any other ideas you might have for something fun to do instead."

"But I want to go to the party!"

"Yes, that does seem like a good time. I understand what a hard decision this is. I know you'll do the right thing by standing in virtuous places because you are such a good young man (soft hand on shoulder). I have confidence in you. What else could you do where you could still have fun and be in a wholesome environment?"

"I could make sure his parents are there."

"That's a great idea, but I still don't feel comfortable with what will be going on."

(Silence.)

"Would you like some ideas?"

(A grunt and shrug of the shoulder.)

"Would you like to go with us to the movies?"

"No way. You're boring. I want to be with my friends."

"Okay, then. Would you like to go bowling or play laser tag with other friends? How about Juan and Tyler and some guys from your swim team?"

"Maybe."

"You could do that or maybe invite them over to our house."

"It won't be as fun."

"What would make it fun?"

"I don't know . . . maybe good food and games."

"Great ideas. Let us know if you want to do the bowling option or hanging out here. If it's our house, I'll order the pizza and dad will work with you on games."

That sounded vastly different than the parent who approaches the child and says, "I heard about the party tonight. You can forget about going. There are no responsible adults in that house, and those kids have a reputation for drinking and immorality." End of conversation (although that couldn't be described as a conversation since it was one sided . . . it was more like a dictate). If a child is resistant to discussing the issue in a sit-down talk, find a less threatening approach. I have discovered that teenagers, particularly young men, are more likely to have a discussion while physically engaged. They might prefer "parallel" rather than "face-to-face" talk while they are shooting a basketball, taking a walk, working on a hobby, watching TV, or driving in a car together with their parent. These activities need to be so natural and frequent between parent and child that the critical conversation becomes an appendage to an already established bond.

Imagine Mosiah's self-governance philosophy guiding a parent's actions. How would children feel growing up in a home that valued accountability and personal responsibility? We see in Mosiah's kingdom that the people rejoiced exceedingly at being set at liberty to account for their own actions and have their voices heard (see Mosiah 29:39). Do we hold family councils and one-on-one interviews? Do we create homes where our children's voices are heard and we listen to their concerns with sincere regard? Mosiah's new rule is an archetype for parenting. We can insert ourselves and our children into this model. The likely outcome? Children will "wax strong in love" toward their parents; they will "esteem

[them] more than any other man" (Mosiah 29:40). What a glorious principle to guide our parenting!

Parenting principles from God and Adam and Eve: We must honor the eternal gift of agency. When governing our children, we should give them appealing choices within reasonable boundaries and accountability for those choices. Each child's feelings should be validated. When resolving conflicts we need to ask, gather information, and listen, listen, listen.

NOTES

1. Ezra Taft Benson, "What I Hope You Will Teach Your Children About the Temple," *Ensign*, August 1985, 8.

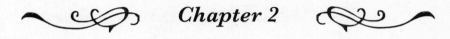

Chapter 2

JESUS WITH JUDAS AND MARY: THE POWER OF DOCTRINE

In the first part of chapter 12 in the book of John, we read an account of Christ's final supper with Mary and Martha in Bethany. Jesus had recently restored their brother Lazarus to life, and he returned to these grateful siblings before his triumphal entry into Jerusalem. Can you envision the feelings these three must have had at that final supper? How would you have felt if you were Mary and Jesus had brought your brother back from the tomb after three days of certain death? What if you were Lazarus? There are not enough "thank yous" or words to describe the depth of gratitude for the Savior and Redeemer.

In fact, Mary *did not* say anything during the meal as recorded by John but quietly opened up her precious vial of spikenard saved for the ritual of burial. Perhaps she was one of the few who appreciated that Christ would soon sacrifice his life for mankind. In a pre-burial ritual, she used this costly ointment on Jesus's feet and wiped them with her hair. The odor soon filled the house and one of his disciples, Judas, condemned Mary's extravagant actions. He chastised her for not selling this ointment and giving the proceeds to the poor. John editorialized, "This he said, not that he cared for the poor, but because he was a thief, and had the bag, and bare what was put therein" (John 12:6).

This scenario is a type for families who have similar experiences around the supper table or elsewhere. Have you had a child who was critical or jealous of his or her sibling and expressed it with an uncharitable complaint? Mosiah warned parents, "Ye will not suffer your children . . . that they transgress the laws of God, and fight and quarrel one with another, and serve the devil, who is the master of sin, or who is the evil spirit which hath been spoken of by our fathers, he being an enemy to all righteousness" (Mosiah 4:14).

Christ, the perfect father, is dealing with a bickering child and his restraint in this situation and response to both "children" speaks volumes. He did not openly punish Judas for his treachery and hypocrisy, nor make an example of him in front of the "family." Instead, Jesus recognized Mary's sacrifice and pure heart. "Let her alone: against the day of my burying hath she kept this" (John 12:7). He praised her benevolence while using it as an example to teach the wayward child. Later, when appropriate, parents should correct serious concerns with children in private (see chapter 5).

We learn from Christ's example that focusing just on the bad behavior is not as effective and can have contrary results. Note that he did not compare ("Why can't you be more like her?") or address Judas's thieving motives in public. Rather, he taught doctrine: "For the poor always ye have with you; but me ye have not always" (John 12:8). In essence, he admonished, "Do not criticize your 'sister.' She has saved this precious ointment for my burial. I will soon sacrifice my body and die for each of you and atone for the sins of the world. She is expressing a grateful heart through service."

Boyd K. Packer gave some extraordinary counsel that should elevate our parenting practices. He said, "True doctrine, understood, changes attitudes and behavior. The study of the doctrines of the gospel will improve behavior quicker than the study of behavior will improve behavior."[1] Alma found this to be true as well: "And now, as the preaching of the word had a great tendency to lead the people to do that which was just—yea, it had had more powerful effect upon the minds of the people than the sword or anything else, which had happened unto them—therefore Alma thought it was expedient that they should try the virtue of the word of God" (Alma 31:5). Putting Elder Packer's and Alma's words into practice as well as following Christ's example is fundamental to righteous parenting.

What was the wrongful behavior in the Mary/Judas scenario Jesus could have focused on? Hypocrisy, maliciousness, and greed.

What was the doctrine Jesus chose to teach instead? Service, sacrifice, the Atonement, gratitude, and love.

What does this do for the family? It lifts the conversation and behavioral expectation. Jesus ignored the subterfuge and used the opportunity to teach the family true doctrine to improve behavior.

At that same table in another family setting, Jesus used a similar approach with a judgmental sister. Martha "cumbered" herself by preparing and serving the food while her sister, Mary, sat at Jesus's feet to hear his words. Martha expressed her love for Christ through service; Mary savored the moments of learning with the Savior. Both sisters were right. Jesus let Martha serve as was her disposition until she became critical of Mary. Martha felt the weight of the work and openly censured Mary's choice and Jesus for not seeming to appreciate her single-handed efforts. She appealed, "Lord, dost thou not care that my sister hath left me to serve alone? Bid her therefore that she help me" (Luke 10:40).

Repeating the pattern of righteous parenting, Christ showed the way to see the positive, ignore the incidental negatives, and teach doctrine in conflicting situations. He said, "Martha, Martha . . ." (I imagine a sympathetic eye and a shake of the head), "thou art careful and troubled about many things" (Luke 10:41). He acknowledged her good intentions. She wanted to be recognized—this invisible servant—and Christ responded. However, he did not publicly reprimand her harsh judgment of Mary. Instead, he focused on the lasting choice of Mary. "But one thing is needful: and Mary hath chosen that good part, which shall not be taken away from her" (Luke 10:42). At a time when Christ was teaching doctrine, it was "needful" to be at his feet. If we nourish ourselves with true manna from heaven, it "will not be taken away from [us]" unlike fleeting food. Christ taught that worldly cares, like our daily bread, often distract us from spiritually eating the Bread of Life.

Focusing on bad behavior is easy for parents to do. We want to pull out the weeds. However, if the plant is too tender and its roots too vulnerable, we can rip out the young plant along with the weeds. Nourishing with doctrine takes great self-control and longitudinal perspective. There are many times when I've had to stop myself in downward spiraling disagreements with my children. "Why can't I see that movie?" "Why can't I wear this to church?" To the latter question, I find it ineffective to say, "The hem is too short" or "That fabric is too revealing" or we get into a debate over inches and stitching. Instead, I have to search for doctrinal moorings to keep us afloat: "One day you will enter the temple, the house of God. This life is to prepare to meet God face to face and the temple is a 'practice' session. We prepare now by wearing clothing that would be in harmony with what we can wear there." If they try to engage me again in discussion, I just repeat some form of the doctrinal answer (with a smile on my face, of course) such as, "Modesty is an outward expression of reverence."

My mother often taught us the doctrinal "whys" of virtuous living. I remember disputing an earlier-than-midnight curfew since my high school friends and I enjoyed attending the midnight showing of movies. Her succinct answer drove truth to a point: "Because the Holy Ghost goes to bed at midnight." The meaning was clear, and I couldn't argue any further.

Elder Lynn G. Robbins summarized the principles Christ lived by teaching us to cultivate the "being" of discipleship more than the "doing." *Being* is doctrinally based; *doing* is behaviorally based:

> When children misbehave, let's say when they quarrel with each other, we often misdirect our discipline on what they *did,* or the quarreling we observed. But the *do*—their behavior—is only a symptom of the unseen motive in their hearts. We might ask ourselves, "What attributes, if understood by the child, would correct this behavior in the future? Being patient and forgiving when annoyed? Loving and being a peacemaker? Taking personal responsibility for one's actions and not blaming?"[2]

These qualities of "being" encourage our children to develop Christlike attributes:

- "You were very kind to invite Teresa to play when she was standing alone."

- "I know how hard it was to tell the truth. Christ taught us to be honest, and you followed His example. Having integrity will bring you peace."

- "Thank you for rocking the baby when she was crying. You have such compassion for others."

Finally, we need to examine whether a child is misbehaving, perhaps like Martha, because they feel misunderstood and underappreciated. It is easy for a parent not to put energy and time into children who are doing well. If there are no problems to manage, what a relief! We tend to ignore children when they are behaving but jump in when they are not. The adage "the squeaky wheel gets the grease" reminds us that children who are creating problems often get more of our attention. That should not be the case! Those who are making good choices should garner more of our encouragement so we increase the likelihood of that behavior to continue. I like to call this "Catch the child being good." Accordingly, we need to be proactive when looking for those moments when we can make positive connections with an otherwise discouraged child. When consciously applied, this parenting strategy works wonders!

Parenting principles from Christ with Judas and Mary: Focus on the positive we see in our children. Teach doctrine when guiding and correcting children. Our efforts should emphasize their character and motives (the "being") rather than just their actions (the "doing").

NOTES

1. Boyd K. Packer, "Little Children," *Ensign,* November 1986, 17.

2. Lynn G. Robbins, "What Manner of Men and Women Ought Ye to Be?" *Ensign,* May 2011, 104.

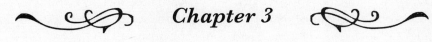

Chapter 3

LEHI AND THE TREE OF LIFE:
THE POWER OF GOOD CHEER

Lehi's vision of the tree of life is truly a story of family. Each of his children are embedded in this vivid vision against the backdrop of "numberless concourses of people" (1 Nephi 8:21). Their choices are what stand out to Lehi as the pinnacle of purpose for his vision. Once Lehi found the tree and ate of the fruit, he described his reaction thus: "The fruit . . . filled my soul with exceeding great joy; wherefore, I began to be desirous that my family should partake of it also; for I knew that is was desirable above all other fruit" (1 Nephi 8:12). The fruit, which was "desirable to make one happy" and was "most sweet" and "white, to exceed all the whiteness that [he] had ever seen," represented the love of God (see 1 Nephi 8:10–11). When we have experienced that joy for ourselves, like Lehi, the first thing we want is that same blessing for our family.

After Lehi turned about to find his family, he saw them at the head of the river that led to the tree. He discovered they were confused, not knowing how to proceed. Lehi's next actions show us exemplary parenting in this family drama. It would seem natural for him to run to his wife and children, to push and cajole them along, to grab their hands and clasp them around the rod that led to the tree. He knew the way. He had passed the test of blinding darkness (see 1 Nephi 8:7–10) and made it to the light. On the contrary, he stayed by the tree of true nourishment. He knew in order to strengthen his family he must strengthen himself and stay close to God. *We must never leave the tree.*

Lehi beckoned to his family since they were a long way off. He had to call loudly so they could find him among the distractions and confusion to find the tree and partake of the fruit. Sometimes our voices must be raised in courage for what is right. Our children need to hear a clear voice when discussing gospel matters. They need to hear unwavering testimonies and love spoken for one another more often. We need more parents who are not afraid to say "no." We should stand firm and warn adolescents entering dangerous domains of immorality. Elder Boyd K. Packer described the moral and spiritual environment parents struggle to preserve in their homes. He said, "We have both the *right* and the *obligation* to raise a warning voice."[1]

My sister-in-law practices this continually as she raises her three teenage children. For example, when her daughter entered middle school, she was confronted with friends who began experimenting in very inappropriate activities. This daughter was invited to an ice skating party by one of these friends, but her mother did not know the kids very well and did not feel good about her daughter going. My sister-in-law told her daughter she couldn't go because of these reasons. Even though her daughter was unhappy not to be included in this newly-formed group of friends, she found out later the kids did very little ice skating and engaged in immoral activities instead. She told her mother later how relieved she was not to have gone.

As Elder Larry R. Lawrence reminds us, we also need to be courageous enough to say "yes" to our children:

> It takes courage to gather children from whatever they're doing and kneel together as a family. It takes courage to turn off the television and the computer and to guide your family through the pages of the scriptures every day. It takes courage to turn down other invitations on Monday night so that you can reserve that evening for your family. It takes courage and willpower to avoid overscheduling so that your family can be home for dinner.[2]

Lehi's example at the tree shows us that to be parents, we must lead and allow others to choose. Christ said, "Come, follow me" and led by example. Lehi stood by the tree with outstretched hand and offered the love he found from the fruit therein. Then, he watched and waited as each child made his choice. No one was forced to the tree. No coercion exists in the Lord's plan, and "God will force no man to heav'n."[3] Each family member was given the opportunity to struggle and grow stronger as they fought his or her way through the darkness with father Lehi offering guidance. Lehi knew that to each is given the gift of agency. As a parent, he could not interfere in the process of spiritual maturation. By the very act of pressing forward, Lehi's family experienced opposition as they progressed toward the tree. Accordingly, only through resistance do we gain strength. Elder Matthew O. Richardson taught about agency:

> Those who teach after this manner of the Spirit help others by inviting, encouraging, and providing them opportunities to use their agency. Parents, leaders, and teachers realize they cannot feel *for,* learn *for,* or even repent *for* their family, congregation, or class members. Rather than asking, "What can I do for my children, class members, or others?" they ask, "How do I invite and help those around me to learn for themselves?" Parents who mirror the workings of the Holy Ghost create homes where families learn to value rather than just learn about values. In like manner, rather than just talking about doctrines, teachers help learners understand and live gospel doctrines. The Holy Ghost is unrestrained as individuals exercise *their* agency appropriately.[4]

Lehi's wife, Sariah, and two of his sons, Nephi and Sam, chose the path and persisted to the tree. Unfortunately, Laman and Lemuel, his two eldest sons, turned away. These two sons' wickedness did not diminish the love Lehi continued to share with them nor the blessings he and Sariah were entitled to receive as righteous parents. Elder Robert D. Hales shared this comforting message:

> We too must have the faith to teach our children and bid them to keep the commandments. We should not let their choices weaken our faith. Our worthiness will not be measured according to their righteousness. Lehi did not lose the blessing of feasting at the tree of life because Laman and Lemuel refused to partake of its fruit. Sometimes as parents we feel we have failed when our children make mistakes or stray. Parents are never failures when they do their best to love, teach, pray, and care for their children. Their faith, prayers, and efforts will be consecrated to the good of their children.[5]

Elder Boyd K. Packer bore witness of the personal insight he gained as he read the story of Lehi's vision:

I read that the prophet Lehi partook of the fruit of the tree of life and said, "Wherefore, I began to be desirous that my family should partake of it also; for I knew that it was desirable above all other fruit" [1 Nephi 8:12]. I had read that more than once. It did not mean much to me. The prophet Nephi also said that he had written "the things of my soul . . . for the learning and the profit of my children" [2 Nephi 4:15]. I had read that before, and it did not mean all that much to me, either. But later when we had children, I understood that both Lehi and Nephi felt just as deeply about their children as we feel about our children and grandchildren. . . . I learned that anyone, anywhere, could read in the Book of Mormon and receive inspiration. Some insights came after reading a second, even a third time and seemed to be "likened" to what I faced in everyday life.[6]

What a statement! Elder Packer initially did not find much relevancy as he read some scriptural passages. These did not come until he had experiences as a parent. With consistent study, he began to identify with mothers and fathers that had lived beyond the pages. I imagine he saw himself standing by the tree as did Lehi and feeling the same desire for his own children to partake of the fruit. From this latter-day Apostle, we learn to continually seek inspiration depending on our present perspective and ability to understand. Have the scriptures become a parenting guide for you? Have you ever read a familiar passage when a verse jumped out with new inspiration and you thought, "Hey, that wasn't in there before!" The scriptures haven't changed—*we* have! The Lord knows how to deliver truth in different packages, depending on our needs and desires. Likewise, our children need different consideration during different stages of their lives. In short, we need to be avid readers of the scriptures and listeners to the Spirit.

Father Lehi's timeless example of patriarchal compassion toward righteous and unrighteous children has immeasurable worth to Latter-day Saint parents. He demonstrated divine love and endless effort to persuade his rebellious sons in spite of the fact *he knew* they would continue in wickedness. As a prophet, Lehi saw the future and the choices his children and posterity would make. After being shown the vision of the tree of life and Laman's and Lemuel's rejection of the love of God, Lehi gathered his sons around him, and "he did exhort [his children] with all the feeling of a tender parent, that they would hearken to his words, that perhaps the Lord would be merciful to them" and "he bade them to keep the commandments of the Lord" (1 Nephi 8:36–38). Unlike his sons with hard hearts, Lehi's parent-heart is described as "tender" or soft, full of charity toward those who treated him contemptuously.

As this conflicted family crossed the ocean, Nephi wrote of the anguish his older brothers brought upon their parents: "Because of their grief and much sorrow, and the iniquity of my brethren, they were brought near even to be carried out of this time to meet their God; yea, their grey hairs were about to be brought down to lie low in the dust; yea, even they were near to be cast with sorrow into a watery grave" (1 Nephi 18:18). Rebellious children can have such a devastating effect on their parents whose only desire is to see their family united. Here is a lesson for any parent who finds him- or herself in such a terrible time. The only parent who fails is the one who loses hope and gives up. Lehi did neither.

As he blessed his family before he died, Lehi prophesied again concerning the wickedness of his Lamanite posterity (see 2 Nephi 1:10–22). Nevertheless, his last words to his rebellious sons were full of hope and anxiety for them: "And that my soul might have joy in you, and that my heart might leave this world with gladness because of you" (1 Nephi 1:21). This sounds like a parent who will never give up hope even though he knows the outcome already. He continued with these rousing words: "Awake, my sons; put on the armor of righteousness. Shake off the chains with which ye are bound, and come forth out of obscurity, and arise from the dust" (1 Nephi 1:23). Again we read that Lehi desires his heart to be filled with cheer, or gladness, by reason of his children.

I can imagine his whole frame shaking as he delivered this impassioned speech. Here is a father with perfect love and faith in his children and in the Lord's plan for his family, even for those heading down the road of destruction. I have always wondered why he pled with them up until the end of his life when he knew they would not repent. Wouldn't that be a good time to let them go and avoid any further personal distress? I believe he did not because a parent who has tasted the fruit of the tree of life and is true to his stewardship will always stand firm. They will never give up. They will beckon to those they love, even . . . no, *especially* to wayward children. I find great comfort in the following statement by Elder Orson F. Whitney:

> The Prophet Joseph Smith declared—and he never taught more comforting doctrine—that the eternal sealings of faithful parents and the divine promises made to them for valiant service in the Cause of Truth, would save not only themselves, but likewise their posterity. Though

some of the sheep may wander, the eye of the Shepherd is upon them, and sooner or later they will feel the tentacles of Divine Providence reaching out after them and drawing them back to the fold. Either in this life or the life to come, they will return. They will have to pay their debt to justice; they will suffer for their sins; and may tread a thorny path; but if it leads them at last, like the penitent Prodigal, to a loving and forgiving father's heart and home, the painful experience will not have been in vain. Pray for your careless and disobedient children; hold on to them with your faith. Hope on, trust on, till you see the salvation of God.[7]

The Apostle Paul's maritime voyage to Rome is a metaphor for the parenting journey we all take in life. Through his example, we learn to warn children of danger, to allow them to make choices and suffer consequences if necessary, to be patient, and to "be of good cheer." As with Lehi, he embodies every good gift parents should seek after diligently.

In Acts 27:8, Paul, the prisoner, and the ship's crew ported in the city of Lasea. The sailors were delayed for some unknown reason, and the season for smooth sailing had passed. From Paul's experience and wisdom, he admonished the crew not to set sail. He was not afraid to speak up to warn them of future perils: "Sirs, I perceive that this voyage will be with hurt and much damage, not only of the lading and ship, but also of our lives" (v. 10). We too must caution our children from navigating into dangerous waters. Like some teenagers who think they know better than their elders, the crewmembers disregarded Paul's warning and set sail nonetheless.

Softly blowing southern winds portended favorable conditions, but soon after the ship passed the isle of Crete, "there arose against it a tempestuous wind" (v. 14). Many terrible consequences followed. The storm tossed the ship so violently the crew was forced to relinquish control. The ship threatened to run aground in a sandbar. The sailors had to lighten the ship by tossing valuable items overboard. Such consequences typify what our children might experience from bad judgment and sin. Moreover, in this perilous state, "neither sun nor stars" appeared for many days and "all hope . . . was then taken away" (v. 20). Likewise, the heavens may be closed to our children as their "celestial navigation" is withheld during a dark period. It tries our very souls to see our children flounder!

In the harrowing stories of Paul and Lehi, we learn that to be patient is to be wise. Our travails in mortality are but tutors; we must allow each person to experience and learn. Acts 27:21 begins, "But after long abstinence," which is the crux of this account. Paul abstained from harsh judgment throughout the ordeal, even though he suffered the effects of others' poor choices. He exercised patience and allowed others to learn from their mistakes. As with any good parent, he did not abandon them but sought for the Spirit and called out encouragement. The Apostle stood in the midst of the crew and said, "I exhort you to be of good cheer: for there shall be no loss of any man's life among you. . . . Wherefore, sirs, be of good cheer" (vv. 22, 25).

Thereafter, Paul nourished the weary crew with meat, saying, "This day is the fourteenth day that ye have tarried and continued fasting, having taken nothing. Wherefore I pray you to take some meat: for this is for our health: for there shall not an hair fall from the head of any of you" (vv. 33, 34). Like a steadfast parent, Paul temporally, emotionally, and spiritually nourished others. He continued to give them hope in their dire circumstances. When the sailors all received nourishment from Paul, their spirits were buoyed; they were "all of good cheer" (v. 36).

Lehi was of good cheer because he understood the Lord's plan. He knew God's promises were sure. Said Lehi, "Notwithstanding our afflictions, we have obtained a land of promise, a land which is choice above all other lands; a land which the Lord God hath covenanted with me should be a land for the inheritance of my seed" (2 Nephi 1:5). This promised land represented two rewards: the temporal one in the Americas and the eternal one in the kingdom of God. We can have the same vision for our families today as we stand by the tree of life. Nourishing, encouraging, and giving hope to our children, especially in their darkest hour, will help them move forward to the light of the Atonement. All will not be lost if we are sealed as families in the temple.

Parenting principles from Lehi: Parents must constantly nourish themselves with the good word of God and His love before they can reach out effectively to their families and lead by example. We must allow children to use their agency in their journey toward eternal life. Never give up on a child, even if they continue to rebel. Our earthly experience is just one part in the plan of eternal progression. If we keep these truths in mind, we can "be of good cheer."

NOTES

1.   Boyd K. Packer, "Our Moral Environment," *Ensign*, May 1992, 67.

2.   Larry R. Lawrence, "Courageous Parenting," *Ensign*, November 2010, 100.

3.   "Know This, That Every Soul Is Free," *Hymns*, no. 240.

4.   Matthew O. Richardson, "Teaching After the Manner of the Spirit," *Ensign*, November 2011, 95.

5.   Robert D. Hales, "With All the Feelings of a Tender Parent: A Message of Hope to Families," *Ensign*, May 2004, 88.

6.   Boyd K. Packer, "The Book of Mormon: Another Testament of Jesus Christ," *Ensign*, May 2005, 7.

7.   Orson F. Whitney, as cited by Boyd K. Packer, "Our Moral Environment," *Ensign*, May 1992, 68; original quote in Conference Report, April 1929, 110.

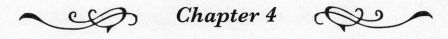

Chapter 4

ALMA AND AMULEK: THE POWER OF FAITH

Alma and Amulek were an incredible missionary companionship. Their discourse covered in Alma chapters 32–34 is worthy of review. They gathered the poor, outcast Zoramites and taught them great truths on the hill Onidah: true worship is not confined to walls of synagogues, humility is an attribute we should seek willingly instead of being compelled to acquire, and faith should be planted and nourished like a seed. Faith is the first principle of the gospel and a foundational parenting principle as well. Faith is a verb. Each action we take is based on our belief in some desired—but unseen—outcome. Spencer W. Kimball expressed it this way:

> Remember that Abraham, Moses, Elijah, and others could not see clearly the end from the beginning. They also walked by faith and without sight.
>
> Remember again that no gates were open; Laban was not drunk; and no earthly hope was justified at the moment Nephi exercised his faith and set out finally to get the plates. . . .
>
> Remember that there were no clouds in the sky, no evidence of rain, and no precedent for the deluge when Noah built the ark according to commandment. There was no ram in the thicket when Isaac and his father left for Moriah for the sacrifice. Remember there were no towns and cities, no farms and gardens, no homes and storehouses, no

blossoming desert in Utah when the persecuted pioneers crossed the plains.

And remember that there were no heavenly beings in Palmyra, on the Susquehanna, or on Cumorah when the soul-hungry Joseph slipped quietly into the grove, knelt in prayer on the river bank, and climbed the slopes of the sacred hill.[1]

And we must remember there are no guarantees of what a child will become when we commit to raising him or her. It is truly an act of faith and love to take an infant, utterly unfamiliar at birth—a stranger, really—and welcome it into our homes and parent it for the rest of our lives. Subsequently, we will examine the correlation between faith and parenthood.

The writer of Hebrews stated, "Now faith is the substance of things hoped for, the evidence of things not seen" (Hebrews 11:1). We can examine this scripture through the lens of parental practices. We hope and we believe in our children. We raise them from infancy, not having any evidence of who or what they will become as they grow. We exercise faith every day that as we nourish our "seed," it will bear fruit one day. In the same chapter of Hebrews, we read about many Old Testament parents who practiced faith in monumental ways:

> By faith Noah, being warned of God of things not seen as yet, moved with fear, prepared an ark to the saving of his house. (v. 4)

> Through faith also Sara herself received strength to conceive seed, and was delivered of a child when she was past age, because she judged him faithful who had promised. (v. 11)

> By faith Abraham, when he was tried, offered up Isaac: and he that had received the promises offered up his only begotten son. (v. 17)

> By faith Isaac blessed Jacob and Esau concerning things to come. (v. 20)

> By faith Jacob, when he was a dying, blessed both the sons of Joseph; and worshipped, leaning upon the top of his staff. (v. 21)

> By faith Moses, when he was born, was hid three months of his parents . . . and they were not afraid of the king's commandment. (v. 23)

With most major endeavors in life, we never have all the answers. Faith, Alma explained, is not a perfect knowledge (see Alma 32:26). In other words, we cannot be perfect people or parents all at once or know everything precisely. Many trips and falls and much trial and error greet us on our walk by faith. That is a comforting concept as a parent of God's children. He trusts us and allows us to experiment with godlike attributes in the perfect "laboratory" of a family unit.

Alma exhorted the Zoramites to "exercise a particle of faith, yea, even if ye can no more than desire to believe . . . even until ye can give place for a portion of my words" (Alma 32:27). He challenged us to plant a seed—a particle of faith we can experiment with like a plant—to see if it grows or not. At the end of verse 27, he asked us to "give place," or in other words, "make room," for a portion of his words. We can crowd our time with temporal tasks and have little left for personal and family scripture study. We can fill our garden with many beautiful plants, but there would be no room for the tree of life. We can engage in many worthwhile activities but must keep our eternal priorities. Elder Dallin H. Oaks gave an excellent conference talk on the subject of choosing between good, better, or best:

> In choosing how we spend time as a family, we should be careful not to exhaust our available time on things that are merely good and leave little time for that which is better or best. A friend took his young family on a series of summer vacation trips, including visits to memorable historic sites. At the end of the summer he asked his teenage son which of these good summer activities he enjoyed most. The father learned from the reply, and so did those he told of it. "The thing I liked best this summer," the boy replied, "was the night you and I laid on the lawn and looked at the stars and talked." Super family activities may be good for children, but they are not always better than one-on-one time with a loving parent.
>
> The amount of children-and-parent time absorbed in the good activities of private lessons, team sports, and other school and club activities also needs to be carefully regulated. Otherwise, children will be overscheduled, and parents will be frazzled and frustrated. Parents should act to preserve time for family prayer, family scripture study, family home evening, and the other precious togetherness and individual one-on-one time that binds a family together and fixes children's values on things of eternal worth. Parents should teach gospel priorities through what they do with their children.[2]

I affirm the sentiments expressed by the father and son in his story. We had an extended family reunion in California with fun-filled days of amusement parks, the beach, and swimming. However, on Sunday we honored the holy day, went to church, visited temple grounds, and held a family devotional and talent show with the cousins, aunts, uncles, and grandparents. At the end of the week, my mom asked my children what was their favorite part. As much as the amusement parks were fun and good, they all agreed they loved the Sunday family night best. We need to be careful in our selection of what is best for our children, not just on vacations, but in our everyday schedules. It is easy to become overwhelmed with opportunities, choices, and competing demands and expectations for our children to partake in so many activities and excel in so many fields. Saying "no" to some good things to preserve the best fosters healthy children and families. There are many "good" branches on a tree, but they must be pruned in order for the trunk and main branches to achieve their full potential.

Alma's discourse on planting and nourishing the seed refers to faith. However, the metaphor for raising children is striking. Children are like seeds—they were spiritually created before being physically created; their full potential is present at birth; they respond to nourishment and protection; they contain reproductive powers; and each seed eventually produces a unique plant. Indeed, in the parable of the tares of the field, Christ compared seeds to children: "The field is the world; the good seed are the children of the kingdom" (Matthew 13:38).

I was concerned about a particular teenager for a period, and one day I was reading Alma 32. The Spirit prompted me to insert "child" for "seed"/"word"/"tree" in this analogy. In reading verses 37–43 at the end of chapter 32, I gained light, hope, and understanding:

> And behold, as the [child] beginneth to grow, ye will say: Let us nourish it with great care, that it may get root, that it may grow up, and bring forth fruit unto us. And now behold, if ye nourish it with much care it will get root, and grow up, and bring forth fruit.
>
> And if ye neglect the [child], and take no thought for its nourishment, behold it will not get any root; and when the heat of the sun cometh and scorcheth it, because it hath no root it withers away, and ye pluck it up and cast it out.
>
> Now, this is not because the [child] was not good, neither is it because the fruit thereof would not be desirable; but it is because your ground is barren, and ye will not nourish the [child], therefore ye cannot have the fruit thereof.
>
> And thus, if ye will not nourish the [child], looking forward with an eye of faith to the fruit thereof, ye can never pluck of the fruit of the tree of life.

But if ye will nourish the [child], yea, nourish the [child] as it beginneth to grow, by your faith and diligence, and with patience, looking forward to the fruit thereof, it shall take root; and behold it shall be a [child] springing up unto eternal life.

And because of your diligence and your faith and your patience with the [child] in nourishing it, that it may take root in you, behold, by and by ye shall pluck the fruit thereof, which is sweet above all that is sweet, and which is white above all that is white, yea, and pure above all that is pure; and ye shall feast upon this fruit even until ye are filled, that ye hunger not, neither shall ye thirst.

Then, [parents], ye shall reap the rewards of your faith, and your diligence, and patience, and long-suffering, waiting for the [child] to bring forth fruit unto you.

It was such a powerful experience to look at the passage this way. Take it a step further by rereading the above verses and inserting your child's name. What stood out to me was how the repeated words, "faith," "diligence," and "patience," described parenting precisely. These attributes are particularly essential to parenting stepchildren in blended families or in many adoptive cases. Truly, trust takes time to grow; relationships form in accordance to the law of the harvest.

President Hinckley borrowed the tree/child analogy as well. "Children are like trees. When they are young, their lives can be shaped and directed, usually with ever so little effort. Said the writer of Proverbs, 'Train up a child in the way he should go: and when he is old, he will not depart from it' [Proverbs 22:6]. That training finds its roots in the home."[3]

A corollary statement found in Alma 32:40 warns us of barren consequence if we do not nourish the child, "looking forward with an eye of faith." How can we cultivate an "eye of faith?" This perspective affirms all children are basically good and rely on the nourishment of others. Some parents are guilty of neglect and will reap what they have sown. What addressed my concerns most personally was that through patience and long-suffering, I must wait for the child to develop according to his or her timetable and the Lord's. It will happen "by and by." Elder Robert D. Hales said, "Waiting upon the Lord gives us a priceless opportunity to discover that there are many who wait upon us. Our children wait upon us to show patience, love, and understanding toward them. Our parents wait upon us to show gratitude and compassion. Our brothers and sisters wait upon us to be tolerant, merciful, and forgiving. Our spouses wait upon us to love them as the Savior has loved each one of us."[4]

Elder Neal A. Maxwell said, "Today, some anxious parents seem to insist on constantly pulling up the daisies to see how the roots are doing."[5] Often it takes many seasons before we see the fruited plant: a testimony to grow, blessings to come, answers to prayers, trials to end. We all mature at different rates and cannot be rushed. A redwood tree takes hundreds of years to mature while a maple becomes an adult tree at about twenty years. Yet we sometimes wish children would "grow up" the same, and we become discontented with the laws of nature.

I appreciated Elder David. A. Bednar's insight into raising his family and often not seeing immediate results. It resonated with me and, I believe, with many families. He described the process of persistent parenting as follows:

> Sometimes Sister Bednar and I wondered if our efforts to do these spiritually essential things were worthwhile. Now and then verses of scripture were read amid outbursts such as "He's touching me!" "Make him stop looking at me!" "Mom, he's breathing my air!" Sincere prayers occasionally were interrupted with giggling and poking. And with active, rambunctious boys, family home evening lessons did not always produce high levels of edification. At times Sister Bednar and I were exasperated because the righteous habits we worked so hard to foster did not seem to yield immediately the spiritual results we wanted and expected.
>
> Today if you could ask our adult sons what they remember about family prayer, scripture study, and family home evening, I believe I know how they would answer. They likely would not identify a particular prayer or a specific instance of scripture study or an especially meaningful family home evening lesson as the defining moment in their spiritual development. What they would say they remember is that as a family we were consistent.[6]

The same might be said of us. While we may not recall what our teachers and parents taught us in formal lessons, we remember their caring and persistence. Elder Neil L. Anderson reminded us, "If a child is not listening, don't despair. Time and truth are on your side. At the right moment, your words will return as if from heaven itself. Your testimony will never leave your children."[7] Yes, *time* and *truth* are on our side! These are essential ingredients in the law of the harvest.

Parenting principles from Alma and Amulek: We must make room for the best choices in our lives. Choose children over other worthy pursuits whenever possible. Raising a child is like growing a seed; both need *faith* in realizing their potential. A parent must cultivate an "eye of faith" in raising their child. Additionally, we need to practice patience, long-suffering, diligence, and patience to wait upon the child to grow to fruition.

NOTES

1.   Spencer W. Kimball, *Faith Proceeds the Miracle* (Salt Lake City: Deseret Book, 1972), 11–12.

2.   Dallin H. Oaks, "Good, Better, Best," *Ensign*, November 2007, 105.

3.   Gordon B. Hinckley, "Four Simple Things to Help Our Families and Our Nations," *Ensign*, September 1996, 7.

4.   Robert D. Hales, "Waiting upon the Lord: Thy Will Be Done," *Ensign*, November 2011, 73.

5.   Neal A. Maxwell, "Remember How Merciful the Lord Hath Been," *Ensign*, May 2004, 44.

6.   David. A. Bednar, "More Diligent and Concerned at Home," *Ensign*, November 2009, 19.

7.   Neil L. Anderson, "Tell Me the Stories of Jesus," *Ensign*, May 2010, 110.

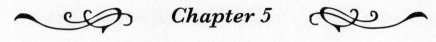

Chapter 5

ALMA AND CORIANTON: THE POWER OF CORRECTING WITH LOVE

Parenting is not a popularity contest. We all want to be liked, especially by our family members, but parents have a solemn stewardship to steer their children in a course correction when needed. Yet so many parents want to avoid the responsibilities of disciplining their children in fear of their children's contempt. In consequence, they become reluctant to reprove their children in order to be *liked.* Too many parents are fearful of their children or doubtful of their own parenting skills. We've all seen this played out in the dreaded grocery store scenario when a parent gives in to the demands of a child who tantrums for candy. It *is* hard to stand firm under the silent stare of others with a screaming child clinging like a barnacle to your leg!

Parents can be confident in Paul's declaration, "I can do all things through Christ which strengtheneth me" (Philippians 4:13). The Lord himself stated the criteria for correcting a child. No power or influence should be exercised except through "persuasion, long suffering, by gentleness and meekness, and by love unfeigned; by kindness, and pure knowledge, which shall greatly enlarge the soul without hypocrisy, and without guile—reproving betimes with sharpness when moved upon by the Holy Ghost; and showing forth afterwards an increase of love toward him whom thou has reproved, lest he esteem thee to be his enemy; that he may know that thy faithfulness is stronger than the cords of death" (D&C 121:41–44). Every principle in these verses is divine guidance for parents and should be evaluated and applied to corrective situations.

The one word to not misunderstand in the prior verses is reproving with *sharpness*. The Lord does not want us to misinterpret its meaning and misapply it. Surely He does not command us to yell sharply after losing our tempers. *Sharpness* in this sense is better understood as "focusing our words and thoughts clearly" like we focus the lens on a camera. If an image in the lens is sharp (or clear), it is in focus. This means we should *choose our words wisely* and not throw them out like sharp spears to wound a tender soul. It may also mean that we select the reproving to have overtones of humor to soften the situation. A well-placed joke can drive home a clear meaning without escalating the conflict. Teenagers especially appreciate subtle humor. After commenting on a child's misbehavior, a parent might smile and say, "Good thing I love you so much!" My friend took a picture of her face wearing an exaggerated unhappy expression and framed it. She kept it on top of the refrigerator, hiding behind boxes. When one of her daughters got out of line, she would say, "Oh dear, it looks like I need to get out my sad face," and she'd pull out the photo of the silly expression. Sometimes she was rewarded with her teenager rolling her eyes and giving the backhanded compliment, "Oh, Mom, you are so weird!" They'd laugh and the tension would dissipate.

Father Lehi chastised Laman and Lemuel for reviling against their brother Nephi for using plain, or clear, words of truth: "And ye have murmured because he hath been plain unto you. Ye say that he hath used sharpness; ye say that he hath been angry with you; but behold, his sharpness was the sharpness of the power of the word of God, which was in him; and that which ye call anger was the truth, according to that which is in God, which he could not restrain, manifesting boldly concerning your iniquities" (2 Nephi 1:26). Here Lehi equates "sharpness" with "boldness"—another good definition and attribute every confident parent should possess. Nephi's brother Jacob also was compelled to use "much boldness of speech" to condemn the wicked (Jacob 2:7).

If we redirect our children with clarity and boldness under the direction of the Spirit, we can more easily follow the next step in the divine corrective process: showing an increase of love afterward. Note that we must show *an increase* of love. Love must already be present to guide the parent-child interaction in order to show forth *more* afterward. In doing so, we "lift up the hands which hang down, and the feeble knees" (Hebrews 12:12). Knowing when and how to show the increase of love that would be most meaningful is left to each parent to determine by the Spirit and the needs of the individual child.

Using a banking metaphor, we make frequent "deposits" when we show and express sincere love to our children. When chastising a child, there must be a secure, accumulated account balance in order for the child to trust the parent. After the correction, the parent adds to the balance to grow the account. If parents follow the pattern in Doctrine and Covenants 121, they are reassured that although "no chastening for the present seemeth to be joyous, but grievous: nevertheless [if love abounds] afterward it yieldeth the peaceable fruit of righteousness unto them which are exercised thereby" (Hebrews 12:11).

An effective way to visualize the corrective process as outlined in Doctrine and Covenants is to use a "sandwich" approach. The two slices of bread are loving statements and affectionate body language. The "meat" of the conversation is the correction. A simplified outline follows of a parent speaking to a child, using the sandwich approach:

Bread: (Look the child in the eye, smile and sit in a relaxed position.) "Jane, I am so grateful for all you do with your siblings. Thank you for fixing dinner last week when Dad and I were out on a date. I really appreciate it."

Meat: "I understand the same night we were gone, your friends came over and you left the house to go to a party where alcohol was served. I am concerned for a couple of reasons. The children were left unattended, and we assumed they were safe with you. We did not know where you were, and we have a rule in our family that everyone must clear their activities first with Dad and me. We wouldn't have approved of that party since these kids have the reputation for underage drinking. It was against the law and, more important, violated the Word of Wisdom, which is a commandment of health and protection from Heavenly Father. Jane, we love you too much to ever allow you to be put in a compromised position where you would be so tempted. Even if you didn't drink, those who are your friends will influence your decisions greatly and perhaps get you in trouble with the law. We need to discuss a consequence." (Discussion follows.)

Bread: (A loving touch or arm around the shoulder) "I know it hurts to have restrictions in your life, but they are just temporary because we have faith in you, Jane. You were sent to our family from a loving Heavenly Father who wants you to be happy and trustworthy. We want to completely trust you again. We love you, and your brothers and sister love you and look up to you. Thank you for being our sweet, wonderful daughter."

Some children won't stick around for a parent to express an increase of love and confidence at this point. Negative consequences have a way of bringing out a very unappreciative child. We are also being tested to see if our "faithfulness is stronger than the cords of death," or at least stronger than an angry child! The words spoken in the final piece of "bread" can be written down and given to the child instead or spoken later when the child is more receptive.

Alma the Younger corrected Corianton using these righteous principles. Corianton was called on a mission to the Lamanites with his brothers Helaman and Shiblon, but he deviated from his duty and fell into lustful temptations. In Alma chapter 39, verses 1–14, Alma elaborated on Corianton's sins and the consequences of his actions. His words are bold and doctrinally-based: "Know ye not, my son, that these things are an abomination in the sight of the Lord . . . ? If ye deny the Holy Ghost when it once has had place in you, and ye know that ye deny it, behold, this is a sin which is unpardonable. . . . I would that ye should repent and forsake your sins, and go no more after the lusts of your eyes. . . . And now the Spirit of the Lord doth say unto me: Command thy children to do good, lest they lead away the hearts of many people to destruction" (Alma 39:5–6, 9, 12).

Alma regretted chastening his son; certainly it is a troublesome thing for any parent. However, Alma spoke as a loving, righteous parent when he said, "I would to God that ye had not been guilty of so great a crime. I would not dwell upon your crimes, to harrow up your soul, if it were not for your good" (Alma 39:7). He set aside his own discomfort and did what was best for his child. "My son, despise not the chastening of the Lord; neither be weary of his correction: For whom the Lord loveth he correcteth; even as a father the son in whom he delighteth" (Proverbs 3:11–12). Love was at the root of Alma's reproof.

The Lord loved the brother of Jared although he chastised him for three hours for neglecting to pray for four years. We read that the brother of Jared received the correction in humility and repented of his transgressions (see Ether 2:14–15). Like the Lord and the brother of Jared, when a parent chastens a child with love, it is an opportunity for the son or daughter to grow in meekness, a divine attribute. "For whom the Lord loveth he chasteneth, and scourgeth every son whom he receiveth. . . . Furthermore we have had fathers of our flesh which corrected us, and we gave them reverence: shall we not much rather be in subjection unto the Father of spirits, and live?" (Hebrews 12:6, 9). Elder D. Todd Christofferson taught, "The invitation to repent is an expression of love. . . . If we do not invite others to change or if we do not demand repentance of ourselves, we fail in a fundamental duty we owe to one another and to ourselves. A permissive parent, an indulgent friend, a fearful Church leader are in reality more concerned about themselves than the welfare and happiness of those they could help."[1]

Alma the Younger preached the mercies of God to his wayward son and showed faith and an increase of love at the end of his interview by calling him to join him and his brethren again in the mission field. I am confident Alma continued vigilant in overseeing his son's activities. Alma's chastisement was effective. Corianton repented and became a great servant in the church. We read later: "Yea, and there was continual peace among them, and exceedingly great prosperity in the church because of their heed and diligence which they gave unto the word of God, which was declared unto them by Helaman, and Shiblon, and Corianton, and Ammon and his brethren, yea, and by all those who had been ordained by the holy order of God, being baptized unto repentance, and sent forth to preach among the people" (Alma 49:30).

We see contrasting examples from other scriptural parents who did not correct or give appropriate consequences to sinful children. Eli, the temple high priest, was father to sons Hophni and Phinehas. These two took the flesh of the sacrificial animals before the fat had been burned at the altar. This is akin to robbing God of a pure sacrifice. Hophni and Phinehas also committed the extremely serious sin of seducing women at the door of the tabernacle. Eli told his sons of their wicked ways but allowed them to continue sinning in their temple duties.

A man of God appeared before Eli and condemned Eli for honoring his sons more than God. He prophesied that Eli and his household would fall to their enemies for their unchecked transgressions before God. He continued, "And this shall be a sign unto thee, that shall come upon thy two sons, on Hophni and Phinehas; in one day they shall die both of them" (1 Samuel 2:34). Nothing is more tragic than the summary heading for 1 Samuel 4: *The Israelites are smitten and defeated by the Philistines, who also capture the ark of God—Eli's sons are slain, Eli dies in an accident, and his daughter-in-law dies in childbirth.* What a sorrowful outcome for this fallen high priest, his family, and the Israelite nation! President Joseph F. Smith taught: "There should [not] be any of us so unwisely indulgent, so thoughtless and so shallow in our affection for our children that we dare not check them in a wayward course, in wrong-doing and in their foolish love for the things of the world more than for the things of righteousness, for fear of offending them."[2]

Our guiding motives should be to fear God more than man; it is wise not to let public opinion control our private practices. We witnessed Christ addressing Judas's faults (see chapter 2) by using the power of positives in Mary's actions (like the two slices of bread in the "sandwich approach"). Punitive public statements and focusing only on bad behavior discourage errant children. Correcting a child is a confidential matter, respecting the feelings of the child and the tender parent-child relationship. I am grateful that in my own deficiencies the penetrating promptings of the Holy Ghost are personal and that no one else knows of God's chastisement but me.

Parenting Principles from Alma and Corianton: Parents have the solemn stewardship to correct erring children. Chastisement should be administered in an unapologetic, yet private and compassionate way, and under the direction of the Holy Ghost. Plenty of positive deposits should be made in the relational "bank account" in order for the necessary chastisement to be most effective. Remember to use doctrine when correcting a child. Whenever disciplining a child, love must be the motivation, and an increase of that godlike love must follow.

NOTES

1. D. Todd Christofferson, "The Divine Gift of Repentance," *Ensign*, October 2011, 39.

2. Joseph F. Smith, *Gospel Doctrine* (Salt Lake City: Deseret Book, 1977), 286.

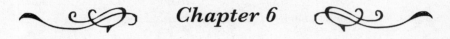

Chapter 6

BETHUEL AND MILCAH:
THE POWER OF SACRIFICE

Bethuel and Milcah are Old Testament parents who are relatively unknown. However, their celebrated daughter is Rebekah, the wife of Isaac. It is thrilling to find parents who define high standards, having raised a virtuous daughter. We discover the results of Rebekah's excellent upbringing during the selection process for Isaac's spouse. Isaac's parents, Abraham and Sarah, are included in this account as they confirm righteous parenting in bringing these two together in marriage. We will focus on the principle of sacrifice these two sets of parents teach us: the sacrifices families should make to prioritize temple marriage and the blessings of sacrifice through work and service.

As mentioned in the introduction, Abraham's idolatrous upbringing necessitated his moving to a new country. The Lord promised that his posterity would become a great nation under which the true priesthood would preside (see Abraham 2:9–10). Abraham's wife, Sarah, was barren for many years until the miraculous birth of her only child, Isaac. Through him, the continuation of the covenant people would be assured.

We spotlight Abraham and Sarah momentarily, for they knew the importance of finding a proper wife for Isaac. Sarah did not entertain the notion of Isaac selecting a wife from the local Canaanite women who were not from the chosen lineage. Isaac was forty years of age and Sarah had died before he pursued a worthy wife. Sarah sacrificed not seeing her son married or enjoying her mortal posterity in order for Isaac to be married under the covenant—in the right place to the right person at the right time.

Abraham commanded his eldest servant, surely a trusted and faithful man, to travel five hundred miles to Haran, the land of Abraham's kindred and covenant people. There he would seek out a handmaiden and bring her home to marry Isaac. The servant, Eleazar, must have taken about three difficult weeks to travel by camel. However treacherous the crossing, this faithful servant continued, not knowing how he would find the chosen wife once he arrived. Yet he trusted the Lord and crafted a plan when he arrived at a well after a long, hot journey. He prayed, "O Lord God of my master Abraham, I pray thee, send me good speed this day, and shew kindness unto my master Abraham. Behold I stand here by the well of water; and the daughters of the men of the city come out to draw water: And let it come to pass, that the damsel to whom I shall say, Let down thy pitcher, I pray thee, that I may drink; and she shall say, Drink, and I will give thy camels drink also: let the same be she that thou hast shewed kindness unto my master" (Genesis 24:12–14).

Eastern customs dictated when someone asked for a drink, the woman drawing water from the communal well would comply. However, each man was responsible for watering his own livestock. Indeed, it would be an enormous task to water the ten camels Eleazer brought. Servants were usually left to complete this chore. In this case, however, Rebekah not only gave Eleazar the desired drink, but she also offered to water his ten camels—the sign Eleazar was seeking. Each camel would drink twenty to thirty gallons of water. The vessel would be dropped and filled and retrieved ten to fifteen times per animal. Rebekah ultimately lifted and lowered the vessel over two hundred times from a hand-drawn well for this stranger. Assuredly, she was not only a beautiful young woman (see Genesis 24:16) but also one who had been taught to follow the Spirit, no matter the inconvenience or how hard the work.

I pause here in the narrative to marvel at how Bethuel and Milcah blessed their daughter by teaching her to go the extra mile in her service and work ethic. Rebekah's extraordinary service was spontaneously given. She was not asked to water all the camels; she offered this sacrifice freely. As a result, Eleazer's prayer was answered, and he knew she was the chosen one for Isaac. Prayer, faith, and following the Spirit were the impetus behind this event, but hard work and service were the direct answer to Eleazar's prayer. This is the pattern of what the Lord expects of us. He requires us to pray in faith, but then to get off our knees and go to work.

What was Rebekah's family's response once Eleazar approached them with a proposition of marriage for their daughter to Isaac? What would yours have been? They answered him, "Behold, Rebekah is before thee, take her, and go, and let her be thy master's son's wife, as the Lord hath spoken" (Genesis 24:51). They realized the sacrifice of Abraham and Sarah in waiting so long and sending this servant so far to find a righteous young woman. They had raised such a daughter and were willing to make an equal sacrifice in sending her far away to live, perhaps never to see her again.

The importance of an eternal marriage under priesthood authority is impressed upon us in this familial biblical story. Elder Russell M. Nelson testified, "I also assert the virtue of a temple marriage. It is the highest and most enduring type of marriage that our Creator can offer His children."[1] To what ends will we go to teach our children to make such sacrifices for the highest of all God's covenants? Indeed, Rebekah was not only willing to go and marry someone she had never met, but would also not even tarry a few days for a celebratory farewell. Eleazar asked to take her immediately. "Hinder me not, seeing the Lord hath prospered my way; send me away that I may go to my master" (Genesis 24:56). Rebekah's family inquired about her wishes in this matter. Her simple reply was, "I will go" (Genesis 24:58). With that singular statement, she became the mother of Esau and Jacob, two great nations, and "the mother of thousands and millions" (Genesis 24:60) under the everlasting covenant.

Sacrificing everything for a temple marriage was impressed upon me during my mission. In the high Altiplano of Bolivia, I lived with a faithful LDS family who lived in humble circumstances, as most did in that region. They were thrilled that the Lima Peru Temple had recently been completed so they could finally be sealed together as husband and wife and as a family. Having a temple closer made the journey possible even if it required much of their precious time and money. They sold all that they could live without, including their wedding bands. Another sister missionary bought the wife's ring; I bought the husband's wedding band. My husband has worn it ever since our wedding day, and it reminds us that even this symbol of marriage means nothing eternally if the ceremony is not performed in the house of God.

Similarly, raising children who know how to work hard and value service requires sacrifice. It is not easy. From my experience, the best way to do this is the way the Lord teaches us: to give us an opportunity, to show us by example, and to praise and encourage us for our efforts and to allow us to feel the joy of doing good. There is no better example in the scriptures than Alma the Younger's counsel to his three sons. When speaking to his middle son, Shiblon, he *praised* the missionary work he had already completed, saying, "I have had great joy in thee already, because of thy faithfulness and thy diligence, and thy patience and thy long-suffering" (Alma 38:3). Alma then *instructed* Shiblon how to persist in the work by giving specific examples throughout chapter 38. He *invited* him, "And now, as ye have begun to teach the word even so I would that ye should continue to teach" (Alma 38:10). Finally, he *encouraged* his middle son's endeavors. "And now, my son, I trust that I shall have great joy in you, because of your steadfastness and your faithfulness unto God; for as you have commenced in your youth to look to the Lord your God, even so I hope that you will continue in keeping his commandments" (Alma 38:2). *Praise and encouragement, opportunity and example.*

In a family unit, we often have the opportunity to teach children how to work when we do it together. We can invite them to work and serve, model how it is done, and praise and encourage them for their efforts. "Have a simple family economy where children have specific chores or household duties and receive praise or other rewards commensurate to how well they do," said Elder M. Russell Ballard. "Help them learn responsibility for their own temporal and spiritual self-reliance."[2] Adam and Eve modeled how to work for their self-sufficiency by tilling the earth and having "dominion over all the beasts of the field" (Moses 5:1). In turn, Cain raised crops, and Abel and was a shepherd (see Moses 5:17).

When we work and serve together, side by side, we develop a relationship with our children and change hearts that we might not affect in any other way. I often take a child or two with me when I am delivering a gift or meal to someone in need. They see the gratitude of the recipient; they feel the immediate joy as we share our love and friendship with others in such a tangible way. I will sometimes say on the way home, "Now, how do you feel inside right now?" and acknowledge the impressions of the Holy Ghost when we are doing good deeds.

President Thomas S. Monson's life has been dedicated to the cause of serving others. Attuned to the gentle impressions of the Spirit and the fruits of helping another, he truly is an example of a sanctified servant-leader.

He witnessed that real joy and lasting happiness can be found in meeting the needs of others: "To find real happiness, we must seek for it in a focus outside ourselves. No one has learned the meaning of living until he has surrendered his ego to the service of his fellow man. Service to others is akin to duty, the fulfillment of which brings true joy."[3]

Ammon discovered the power of changing hearts when he served King Lamoni. Following his capture by the Lamanite guards, Ammon presented himself as a servant to the king. Ammon was put in a disadvantaged situation of protecting the king's sheep by the waters of Sebus with a few other shepherds. It was a popular place for rogue Lamanites to scatter and capture the flock. The enemy approached, outnumbering their little band, and the servants succumbed to fear. Previously, servant-shepherds had lost the flocks and were executed by the king. However, Ammon went the extra mile, as did Rebekah, and did not shrink from the challenge.

Ammon was emboldened by the power of God, his duty to the king, and his desire to "win the hearts" of his fellow servants (Alma 17:29). In a miraculous feat, he beat back the enemy, recovered the flock after they were scattered, and saved their lives.

King Lamoni's servants brought evidence of Ammon's power before the king and he marveled. The king perceived that Ammon was sent from God, was invincible, and was a friend to the king (see Alma 18:1–3). At this point, the king's hardened heart began to change. He began fearing for his past sins and wrongs he had committed. He asked, "Where is this man that has such great power?" (Alma 18:8).

Where *was* Ammon? Resting from the exhausting battle he won singlehandedly? Praying for an opportunity to teach the wicked Lamanites? Writing a letter back home of his conquest? The answer to this question is the crucial piece to true service. The servants responded, "Behold, he is feeding thy horses" (Alma 18:9). Previously, Ammon and the others had been commanded to ready the chariots for the king's journey. Ammon had not let a near-death experience and triumph over the enemy hold in abeyance his station of responsibility.

When the king heard of this faithful servant's undeviating sense of duty, he was even more astonished. "Surely, there has not been any servant among all my servants that has been so faithful as this man; for even he doth remember all my commandments to execute them" (Alma 18:10). Feeding the horses proved to strike the king speechless and prepare his heart to hear the word of God. His countenance had changed! His heart was softened! He couldn't speak for an hour! It is wise to take this same approach with our children. The saying is true: "They don't care how much you know until they know how much you care." Ammon did not begin his mission by preaching; he began it by serving.

A friend shared an example of the tremendous impact of his parents as they sacrificed and served. As a young boy, he grew up with very little. His family was experiencing the residual effects of the Great Depression. His father's schoolteacher paychecks were spread thin for a family of eight. Then, just before December of his eleventh year, his aunt was diagnosed with cancer. His family gathered in a council to decide what to do to help their relatives. They took their saved coins for Christmas, collected them in a jar, and walked it over to their aunt and uncle's house. Even though this meant his family would have nothing, at least their relatives, devastated by disease, could have a small measure of goodness at Christmastime.

In lieu of a Christmas tree, his parents dug up a small evergreen bush, brought it inside in a pot, and decorated it with wrinkled tinsel saved from the previous year. My friend did not care for himself but worried for his younger sisters since there would be no presents that year. So on his own, he rummaged through a neighbor's discarded woodpile and made wooden blocks for them. On Christmas Eve, when he crept up in the bare blackness to put the only presents by the hearth, he heard a scratching of carols on a vinyl record. Soon, two figures emerged—his mother and father dancing. On their faces—joy. They beckoned him to join their circle and he was enveloped by love that night. No Christmas was any sweeter.

Working together can deepen our relationships with each other in ways not otherwise realized. The following is another example of a mother and son bound together in unified, consecrated work. The parents of this teenager were struggling in their parent-child relationship. He challenged them severely, and they were at a loss. His mother prayed for answers and felt impressed to plant a garden. She gave a row of tomatoes to her son to tend, and she spent time by his side as he weeded and cared for them. The safe space she created among those plants opened up his heart. Their time together was uninterrupted and unhurried. They talked. She listened. The tomatoes were secondary to what was being tended. They grew closer, and she understood him better. That became a sacred space. Soon after the harvest, this son passed away unexpectedly. How grateful this mother was for that consecrated time together.

Quiet acts of service may not be appreciated by our children all at once, but they can have a lasting effect later in life. Elder James E. Faust shared this story from his childhood:

> As a small boy on the farm during the searing heat of the summer, I remember my grandmother Mary Finlinson cooking our delicious meals on a hot woodstove. When the wood box next to the stove became empty, Grandmother would silently pick up the box, go out to refill it from the pile of cedar wood outside, and bring the heavily laden box back into the house. I was so insensitive and interested in the conversation in the kitchen, I sat there and let my beloved grandmother refill the kitchen wood box. I feel ashamed of myself and have regretted my omission for all of my life. I hope someday to ask for her forgiveness.[4]

I will never forget the emotion as he shared this story in general conference. Decades later, the regret he still felt was palpable, and the gratitude, profound.

When we teach our children to work and contribute to family, their needs are appropriated a little more wisely and their wants are perhaps not quite as critical. They tend to feel less entitled to the latest purchasing whim. Each penny is precious! Our teenagers are responsible for filling the gas tank of the car they drive. It is amazing how they measure the cost of each mile, many times opting to walk or bike instead. Elder Joe J. Christensen gave an outstanding talk about the dangers of entitlement and laziness—the problem attitudes of youth when they are indulged by their parents. He warned,

> We live in a world of entertainment in full color with a lot of fast action, a world in which many children grow up thinking that if it isn't fun, it is boring and not worthwhile. Even in family activities, we need to strike a balance between play and work. Some of my most memorable experiences while growing up centered around family activities: learning how to shingle a roof, build a fence, or working in the garden. Rather than being all work and no play, for many of our children it is almost all play and very little work. As a consequence of overindulgence, many children leave homes ill-prepared to meet the real world. . . . All too many enter marriages who have never learned to cook, sew, or develop other important life skills. Ignorance of these needed skills, along with the lack of understanding of the management of money, sow the seeds for many failures in our children's marriages.[5]

President Hinckley affirmed the value of work within the family and society. "Children need to work with their parents, to wash dishes with them, to mop floors with them, to mow lawns, to prune trees and shrubbery, to paint and fix up, to clean up, and to do a hundred other things in which they will learn that labor is the price of cleanliness, progress, and prosperity. There are too many youth who are growing up with the idea that the way to get something is to steal it."[6]

God declared *His* work does not end. He glories in working on the salvation and exaltation of all His children (see Moses 1:39). Christ taught us how to serve throughout his ministry, concluding at the Last Supper. "He that is greatest among you," he said, "let him be as the younger; and he that is chief, as he that doth serve" (Luke 22:26). Then Christ washed the feet of his disciples to distill his teachings. When Peter saw Christ's humble service before him, he cried out in protest, feeling unworthy of such a loving act. Christ taught him that to be a servant in God's kingdom is a privilege and requirement. Peter's zeal to be fully immersed in service is stirring: "Lord, not my feet only, but also my hands and my head" (John 13:9). That same attitude can be taught to our children: to be a part of our family, we all have the privilege and expectation to fully serve one another.

Parenting principles from Bethuel and Milcah: We must teach our children to make whatever sacrifice necessary to be married in the temple to a worthy spouse. Heavenly Father testifies that work and service are essential to godhood. Parents should set the example of working and giving service, offering their children the opportunity to contribute to family and building personal character. In doing so, their hearts and hands will become united.

NOTES

1. Russell M. Nelson, "Celestial Marriage," *Ensign*, November 2008, 92.

2. M. Russell Ballard, "What Matters Most Is What Lasts Longest," *Ensign*, November 2005, 43.

3. Thomas S. Monson, "The Joy of Service," *New Era,* October 2009, 4.

4.   James E. Faust, "The Weightier Matters of the Law: Judgment, Mercy, and Faith," *Ensign*, November 1997, 59.

5.   Joe J. Christensen, "Greed, Selfishness, and Overindulgence," *Ensign*, May 1999, 10.

6.   Gordon B. Hinckley, "Four Simple Things to Help Our Families and Our Nations," *Ensign*, September 1996, 7.

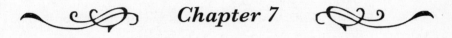

Chapter 7

THE BROTHER OF JARED: THE POWER OF PROPER PERSPECTIVE

I was amused by a computer-generated image in a magazine many years ago. It showed a big, yellow, warning road sign with the large, bold word: "CAUTION" across the top. In slightly smaller print below it warned: "THIS SIGN HAS SHARP EDGES." And then in smaller print below that: "Do not touch the edges of this sign." Finally, at the bottom of the sign, in tiny letters was printed: "Also, the bridge is out ahead." When I showed this funny picture to my son, I said, "There's an important message in there." He agreed. I stated what I thought was obvious: "Read the fine print or you'll be in trouble." He looked a little surprised and replied, "No. That's not it. The message is, 'Don't blow the little things out of proportion.'" After a moment's reflection, I realized his perspective was better than mine. He was saying in essence, "Don't sweat the small or insignificant stuff or you'll overlook what is really important." That was a true-to-life observation from a teenager who sometimes got grief from parents who made a big deal over things that didn't matter all that much.

In parenting, the small stuff can be many things: mistakes common to human nature, immature decision-making skills of children, poor communication and disagreements, small irritations that flare due to stress or fatigue and so forth. We should remember that we are all inadequate for the job as parents and that children are just beginners in life. "Be ye therefore perfect" is an eternal goal, not an earthly finish line. What is a major obstacle to overcome along life's journey? Knowing how to let go and forgive ourselves and others for our frailties. If not, they become insurmountable roadblocks. They grow those "sharp edges" and exaggerated messages on the caution sign.

We take such lessons from the brother of Jared. His journey to the Americas halted at the seashore. After he, his family, and his friends escaped the fall of the Babylonian tower and confounding of languages, they traveled a great distance and harbored for four years in a place called Moriancumer. There, the Lord instructed the brother of Jared to build barges. These barges were sealed on all sides and could travel on the surface of water or submerged, like a submarine. However, there could be no light in this type of vessel. The brother of Jared presented this concern to the Lord, who answered, "What will ye that I should do that ye may have light in your vessels?" (Ether 2:23). This is another profound example of letting a child work through his own solutions and, in so doing, allowing him to gain confidence, experience, and wisdom.

The brother of Jared offered to the Lord sixteen clear stones, two for each of the eight barges. He did not use ordinary rocks, but fashioned a better product the best way he could, which required effort and ingenuity. He moltened the rock until it became clear glass—like diamonds—to resemble or reflect light. The brother of Jared presented the stones and prayed in faith, "I know, O Lord, that thou hast all power, and can do whatsoever thou wilt for the benefit of man; therefore touch these stones, O Lord, with thy finger, and prepare them that they may shine forth in darkness; and they shall shine forth unto us in the vessels which we have prepared, that we may have light while we shall cross the sea" (Ether 3:4).

You may wonder why this man went to all the trouble to make the clear rock. The Lord could have touched any common stones and turned them to light. Why, then? The brother of Jared could never *make* light; he could never be perfect in this thing. However, that did not discourage him. He did all he could to design a light from the resources at hand. Then, he went to the source and giver of light. This he knew: God takes our best efforts—as simple, ordinary, and inadequate as stones—and touches them with His finger. Anything He touches, He blesses and illuminates with His light. As parents, we might say the same prayer: "Touch these my inadequacies, my lack of ability, O Lord, with thy finger, and change me to shine forth in darkness."

The brother of Jared could have felt ashamed at his feeble attempt to re-create light, knowing he could never even approximate the ideal. He might have felt frustrated and given up when his effort was not perfect. The same can be said of parenting. It is difficult not to let our inadequacies overcome us. We need to remember that we are not alone in the quest for perfection. The brother of Jared presented his best, and the Lord magnified him. If we do all we can, it is enough. By keeping that miracle in mind, all things will stay in perspective.

On the other hand, we can easily blow small things out of proportion, like the road sign I showed my son. One way we do this is through unhealthy comparison. Comparing our parenting to other parents can result in an unbalanced view: seeing the best in others and the worst in ourselves. There *is* wisdom in learning from other good parents' examples and adopting inspired practices. Nevertheless, too many parents become discouraged when they dwell on their own deficits with the attitude of: "I will never be as good as . . ." This is an unproductive exercise. By the same token, comparing children to their siblings or to other children often fosters discouragement in the child who can never equal the abilities and nature of others. These futile exercises exasperate an unrealistic expectation in ourselves or our children and blow our vision out of proportion.

Another similar challenge for parents is to not overinflate problems or challenges; instead, we should put them in perspective. Nephi's record in the Book of Mormon is an incredible resource for parents who are feeling discouraged. He wrote about his journey to the promised land many years after they had arrived. In his reflection of their innumerable trials, they shrank into nothingness compared to the blessings. In fact, there is only one cursory line in one verse that barely whispers the trials of that extensive period: "And we did travel and wade through much affliction in the wilderness" (1 Nephi 17:1).

Nephi undoubtedly appreciated the severity of what he and his family had experienced over those eight years in the harsh and barren desert, but he chose to focus on the blessings instead. He followed up that same verse with a specific blessing: "And our women did bear children in the wilderness" (1 Nephi 17:1). He then elaborated on more miracles: they were able to be sustained on raw meat, the mothers had plenty of milk to supply their babies' needs, the women became strong like unto the men, and all were able to bear the burden of the journey without complaint. To summarize their eight years, he chose one verse full of praise for God's mercies and testimony to his children. "And thus we see that the commandments of God must be fulfilled. And if it so be that the children of men keep the commandments of God he will nourish them, and strengthen them, and provide means whereby they can accomplish the thing which he has commanded them; wherefore, he did provide means for us while we did sojourn in the wilderness" (v. 3). He taught us that we need not dwell on our difficulties but find the blessings from them. Nephi presented no more ostensive evidence than in his exposition at the beginning of the Book of Mormon. Summarizing his life, fraught with grief and goodness, he testified: "But behold, I, Nephi, will show unto you that the tender mercies of the Lord are over all those whom he hath chosen, because of their faith, to make them mighty even unto the power of deliverance" (1 Nephi 1:20). Do we profess the same of our lives?

Focusing on the tender mercies in our circumstances and goodness in our children helps us to see the finger of God touching our lives as he did the clear stones. We can look at a particular challenging trait in a child two ways; one is negative, the other is positive. Parents should foster the side that illuminates hope and productivity. One parent might say to a child, "You are so annoying. I wish you wouldn't bother me so much!" A different parent might look at a child with those same attributes and remark, "Boy, you are so persistent! I'm always amazed at how you believe in yourself." Righteous parenting requires us to turn these rough stones into light by seeing the positive in our children.

Negative Trait	Positive Trait
Rowdy, Unruly	Energetic, Full of Life
Timid, Withdrawn	Sensitive, Reflective
Argumentative, Opinionated	Independent, Creative Thinker
Daydreamer, Dawdler	Content, Introspective
Stubborn	Tenacious, Determined
Bossy, Controlling	Confident Leader

When I became discouraged or overwhelmed in a particularly challenging period of parenting, I benefitted by taking a step back. Widening my myopic view, I saw more clearly what was really important, like the small print on the sign that sometimes gets lost in our anxiety. I was still aware of the problem, but I turned it on its head by recounting all the good in that child and all the blessings we had. I saw the challenge in a new way. While sitting in sacrament meeting, I had the distinct impression that my Heavenly Father had enormous confidence in me to entrust me with such a special child. At that moment, my burden turned into joy. I became more grateful for His love and humbled by His trust in me.

This is why prayer is such a divine gift—it teaches us to slow down and focus on gratitude first instead of the problems so our blessings become the priority. Some parents have even experienced such feelings of gratitude during prayer that their heavy hearts feel unburdened and they confess to God, "Never mind. It's not that important anymore. It will be fine." By inviting gratitude into our attitude, we invite the Comforter to speak peace. Counting our blessings daily—even hour-by-hour—is one of the single most powerful parenting tools God has given us.

The Apostle Paul revealed to us his weakness, calling it a "thorn in the flesh" (2 Corinthians 12:7). He prayed many times to have his problems taken away, but they were not. Yet he gained a celestial perspective. Paul described the Lord's response: "And he said unto me, My grace is sufficient for thee: for my strength is made perfect in weakness" (2 Corinthians 12:9). Paul resolved, "Most gladly therefore will I rather glory in my infirmities, that the power of Christ may rest upon me . . . for when I am weak, then am I strong" (2 Corinthians 12:9–10). Paul received a new perspective: challenges can cause us to turn to God and rely on the mercies and strength of the Atonement. When we acknowledge our weaknesses and truly realize we cannot do it alone, we become strong in our dependence and relationship with our Heavenly Father and His son.

What areas of weakness in parenting would you like to turn into strengths? I would suggest writing down impressions you might receive while reading this book. Like Paul, we need to acknowledge first our dependence upon God in all things. Next, pray about and ponder ways you might use the Atonement to give you sufficient strength and grace. I would also suggest talking to your spouse or a trusted friend to whom you can commit making personal goals and regularly report your progress. Journaling your thoughts and actions is another way to track new behaviors and attitudes. Remember that changing incorrect, entrenched habits are not easy to overturn; it requires time, patience, and practice. The discussion questions at the end of this book will help you reflect upon the principles outlined in each chapter. They will be a guide as you increase your ability to improve your parenting practices and find ways you can make course corrections in your approach to raising children in righteousness.

Nephi's honest expressions and tender feelings give parents insights into the process of being patient with our weaknesses and focusing on the positive. Nephi was, at times, beset with despair over his temptations and trials. The section of 2 Nephi 4:17–35 is called the "Psalm of Nephi" because of its poetic structure and musicality. I am so grateful that Nephi included this passage in his book. It is the first glimpse that he was not perfect. Like the brother of Jared, he knew what kind of person he could become, but righteous desire and actual execution can be difficult to reconcile.

Nephi wrote, "O wretched man that I am! Yea, my heart sorroweth because of my flesh; my soul grieveth because of mine iniquities. I am encompassed about, because of my sins . . ." (2 Nephi 4:17–18). Yet Nephi stands out as one of the greatest prophet/parents when he shifts his attitude from fear to faith in the next breath: ". . . nevertheless, I know in whom I have trusted. My God hath been my support; he hath led me through mine afflictions in the wilderness; and he hath preserved me upon the waters of the great deep. He hath filled me with his love, even unto the consuming of my flesh" (2 Nephi 4:19–21). He rallied his spirits for the rest of the chapter, ending in this positive proclamation: "Therefore, I will lift up my voice unto thee; yea, I will cry unto thee, my God, the rock of my righteousness. Behold, my voice shall forever ascend up unto thee, my rock and mine everlasting God. Amen" (2 Nephi 4:35). His perspective changed.

Nephi's brother Jacob also wrote about teaching his brethren and children. In his discourse, he explained, "I will unfold this mystery unto you; if I do not, by any means, get shaken from my firmness in the Spirit, and stumble because of my over anxiety for you" (Jacob 4:18). Concern for our children can grow into overanxiety and become a stumbling block if not kept in balance. We need to check ourselves, like Jacob, and remember that the "battle is not [ours], but God's" (2 Chronicles 20:15). Unhealthy anxiety blows things out of proportion.

My parents' concern for my husband and me ballooned into overanxiety when we announced we were being transferred to Chicago for my husband's work. It was so far away from home. They worried how we would do in this big city all by ourselves. They despaired how little they would see their grandchildren. Their response was so startling that I still remember their exact words. My mom pled, "I beg you with every fiber of my being not to go." My dad tersely warned, "Avoid it like the plague." Yes, they overreacted. It was so uncharacteristic, and I was disheartened. I reminded them that *they* used to live in Illinois—so far from their families—while my dad was finishing his PhD. In case they had forgotten, I reminded them that I had been born there! Without their blessing, my husband and I moved anyway, and it all worked out well. They grew supportive of our decision. Since then, I've reminded my parents about their alarming response, and we've had many laughs over the years.

As you read this book, you might think, "This is too much. I can't do it all." That is true. We cannot do it all or expect perfection in parenting. The principles taught here are the ideal. They are the light emanating through us, the common stones. The key is not to let our weaknesses overwhelm us, but to rejoice in the goodness of God and His tender mercies showered upon us each day. Just pick one or two manageable principles you would like to work on. When those become stronger, focus on another one or two, and so on. Repentance should be applied liberally every day. Remember we are not alone in our efforts. The Lord said, "Fear not, I am with thee, O be not dismayed" (Isaiah 41:10). If we focus on and trust in His divine help, and do our best (even if we produce just pieces of glass), He will fill us with His perfect light.

Parenting principles from the brother of Jared: We need to keep all things in perspective and not let the little problems overwhelm us. We need to have faith, not fear and anxiety. If we do our best, and rely on the mercies of God, He will touch us and make us better than we could be on our own. Let us focus on our blessings, not our problems; let us shift our perspective to the positive, not the negative. These attitudes will guide righteous principles and remind us what is most important.

 **Chapter 8**

CAPTAIN MORONI:
THE POWER OF BANNERS
AND FORTIFICATIONS

A large portion of the book of Alma is filled with battles, deaths, intrigue, wickedness, and the destruction and reconstruction of cities. Accordingly, chapters 43–62 are referred to as the "war chapters." These chapters seem incongruent at first to the teachings of God. Why did Mormon extensively include them and how can they instruct us as parents? We turn to the chief leader during these wars, Captain Moroni, for answers. No parenting discussion is complete without a study of his remarkable life. He was a loyal and courageous countryman and defender of liberty, motivated by love for God and family. We can learn much from this devoted leader and father who is described thus: "Yea, verily, verily I say unto you, if all men had been, and were, and ever would be, like unto Moroni, behold, the very powers of hell would have been shaken forever; yea, the devil would never have power over the hearts of the children of men" (Alma 48:17).

We know all things physical can teach us spiritual lessons. An iron rod can represent the word of God; springtime reminds us of the resurrection; a sacrificial lamb symbolized the Lamb of God. "Wherefore, verily I say unto you that all things unto me are spiritual, and not at any time have I given unto you a law which was temporal; neither any man, nor the children of men; neither Adam, your father, whom I created" (D&C 29:34). Real wars are a physical metaphor for spiritual wars of today. Of this war, Elder Henry B. Eyring warned, "There has been a war between light and darkness, between good and evil, since before the world was created. The battle still rages and the casualties seem to be increasing."[1] Likewise, Elder M. Russell Ballard remarked: "We are in a war. This war is the same war that raged in the premortal world. Lucifer and his followers are committed to an evil direction."[2]

Captain Moroni rallied his people to fight against Amalickiah and the Lamanites who were engaged in perpetual battles against the Nephites. Hoping a visual display would incite patriotism and religious zeal, Moroni ripped his coat. On a piece he wrote: "In memory of our God, our religion, and freedom, and our peace, our wives, and our children" (Alma 46:12). It was called the "title of liberty." He tied this banner to a pole and strode through the cities, waving the flag and calling for Christian people everywhere to enter into a covenant with God. His actions and words had their desired effect, and "people came running together with their armor girded about their loins, rending their garments in token, or as a covenant, that they would not forsake the Lord their God" (Alma 46:21).

In our spiritual war over the preservation of families, we have a seminal standard to wave in declaration of our beliefs. The inspired document "The Family: A Proclamation to the World" is our comparative title of liberty. It declares the true nature of families as boldly, clearly and profoundly as Moroni's message spoke to the Nephites of their duty. Among other things, it declares our parental obligations:

> Husband and wife have a solemn responsibility to love and care for each other and for their children. "Children are an heritage of the Lord" (Psalm 127:3). Parents have a sacred duty to rear their children in love and righteousness, to provide for their physical and spiritual needs, to teach them to love and serve one another, to observe the commandments of God, and to be law-abiding citizens wherever they live. . . .
>
> By divine design, fathers are to preside over their families in love and righteousness and are responsible to provide the necessities of life and protection for their families. Mothers are primarily responsible for the nurture of their children. In these sacred responsibilities, fathers and mothers are obligated to help one another as equal partners.[3]

We are blessed with an abundance of such banners. Our leaders' conference messages are published in a magazine called the *Ensign*—another word for standard or flag. A further declaration called "The Living Christ: The Testimony of the Apostles" was issued to commemorate the second millennium following the Lord's birth. An excerpt follows:

> We bear testimony, as His duly ordained Apostles—that Jesus is the Living Christ, the immortal Son of God. He is the great King Immanuel, who stands today on the right hand of His Father. He is the light, the life, and the hope of the world. His way is the path that leads to happiness in this life and eternal life in the world to come. God be thanked for the matchless gift of His divine Son.[4]

Many families frame these documents and display them in their homes. They become a visual reminder like Moroni's banner. However, Moroni did more than just post his message and walk away; he waved the flag for all to see and called them forth. He also "caused the title of liberty to be hoisted upon *every tower* which was in the land" (Alma 46:36; emphasis added). Likewise, parents in every home should declare and discuss the messages from our prophets and apostles with their children. Righteous parents will invite their children to adopt these principles and examine their own dedication as well. Regarding the proclamation on the family, Elder M. Russell Ballard said,

> It was then and is now a clarion call to protect and strengthen families and a stern warning in a world where declining values and misplaced priorities threaten to destroy society by undermining its basic unit.
>
> The proclamation is a prophetic document, not only because it was issued by prophets but because it was ahead of its time. It warns against many of the very things that have threatened and undermined families during the last decade and calls for the priority and the emphasis families need if they are to survive in an environment that seems ever more toxic to traditional marriage and to parent-child relationships. . . . Today I call upon members of the Church and on committed parents, grandparents, and extended family members everywhere to hold fast to this great proclamation, to make it a banner not unlike General Moroni's "title of liberty," and to commit ourselves to live by its precepts. As we are all part of a family, the proclamation applies to everyone.[5]

Following Moroni's rally to arms, the Nephites took action. The balance of chapters 43–62 details the extensive preparations for war. These descriptions should be read with spiritual eyes to appreciate the trail of truths left streaming for us today. The fortifications, or strongholds, represent our homes and communities in enemy territory. The enemy is Satan and his forces. Alma chapter 50 begins with Moroni not ceasing to make preparations for war, even though they had achieved success in recent battles and were in a relative time of peace. Hence, we cannot afford to rest in our efforts to protect and reinforce our homes.

In a prior battle, Moroni strengthened his strongholds by casting dirt into mounds that served as barriers between them and the enemy. The ridge of earth was elevated so Lamanite stones and arrows could not reach them, nor did any enemy dare to scale it. In fact, the approaching Lamanites were "*astonished exceedingly* because of the wisdom of the Nephites in *preparing their place of security*" (Alma 49:5; emphasis added). In verse 8, it reads, "To their uttermost astonishment, [the Nephites] were prepared for them, in a manner which never had been known among the children of Lehi." Finally, just to make sure we really see the lesson, we read of Amalickiah's chief captains: "[they] durst not attack the Nephites at the city of Ammonihah, for Moroni had altered the affairs among the Nephites, insomuch that the Lamanites were disappointed in their places of retreat and they could not come upon them" (Alma 49:11).

What a powerful parenting description for us! I want to exceedingly astonish and disappoint Satan and his forces with my strongholds so they don't dare attack. Perhaps that means we need to alter our affairs and change our strategies. Maybe we have been too lax in personal and family scripture reading. Perhaps we haven't seen the need for keeping holy all aspects of the Sabbath day. We might regard Sunday more like another day of the week. Perhaps we attend church, but leave it behind when we return home. Could it be that television, gaming systems, electronic devices, and movies are feeding stronger, more persistent messages to our children than our part-time parenting efforts? A prayerful contemplation of our stewardship might reveal how we need to improve in raising our children.

Moroni not only strengthened and protected his people (and family) from without but also from within. They did all they could to build a physical barrier to hedge against the enemy while concurrently fortifying their faith and testimony. We read that he was a man of "perfect understanding," whose heart did "swell with thanksgiving to his God" and "was firm in the faith of Christ" (Alma 48:11–13). His people exercised "faith that by so doing God would prosper them in the land, or in other words, if they were faithful in keeping the commandments of God that he would prosper them in the land" (Alma 48:15). Building *internal* "fortifications" of faith, testimony, gratitude, knowledge, and obedience became a spiritual armor for the righteous. They were putting on the full armor of God of which the Apostle Paul spoke:

> Put on the whole armour of God, that ye may be able to stand against the wiles of the devil. For we wrestle not against flesh and blood, but against principalities, against powers, against the rulers of the darkness of this world, against spiritual wickedness in high places. Wherefore take unto you the whole armour of God, that ye may be able to withstand in the evil day, and having done all, to stand. Stand therefore, having your loins girt about with truth, and having on the breastplate of righteousness; And your feet shod with the preparation of the gospel of peace; Above all, taking the shield of faith, wherewith ye shall be able to quench all the fiery darts of the wicked. And take the helmet of salvation, and the sword of the Spirit, which is the word of God: Praying always with all prayer and supplication in the Spirit, and watching thereunto with all perseverance and supplication for all saints. (Ephesians 6:11–18)

The physical representation of this spiritual principle is found in Alma chapter 43. Moroni "prepared his people with breast-plates and with arm-shields, yea, and also shields to defend their heads, and also they were dressed with thick clothing" (v. 19). In contrast, their Lamanite enemies were exposed to arrows and stones and swords because they were unprepared for battle. They were naked except for a loincloth and carried weapons but no breastplates or shields. The Nephites occasionally fell, but the Lamanites' "nakedness was exposed to the heavy blows . . . which brought death almost at every stroke" (see Alma 43:37–38). "Therefore, they were exceedingly afraid of the armies of the Nephites because of their armor, notwithstanding their number being so much greater than the Nephites" (Alma 43:21). It does not matter the number of Satan's forces if we are well armed and spiritually prepared. They will be exceedingly afraid to attack those who put on the whole armor of God.

While speaking of building a place of safety for our children, another person from the Bible inspires us with her courage and diligence. Jochebed, a complementary character to Moroni, teaches what it means to protect our children from danger. She was the mother of Moses at the time Pharaoh ordered all male children to be killed upon birth in attempt to control the Hebrew population. Elder Robert D. Hales reflected upon this great woman by saying,

The scriptures record, "By faith Moses, when he was born, was hid three months of his parents, . . . and [his parents] were not afraid of the king's commandment." When Moses grew too old to be concealed, his mother, Jochebed, constructed an ingenious basket of bulrushes, waterproofed it with slime and pitch, and placed her son inside. She directed the tiny vessel down the river to a safe place—to where the pharaoh's daughter bathed.

Leaving nothing to chance, Jochebed also sent along an inspired helper, her daughter Miriam, to keep watch. When Pharaoh's daughter, the princess, found the baby, Miriam bravely offered to call a Hebrew nurse. That nurse was Jochebed, Moses' mother.

Because of her faithfulness, Moses's life was spared. In time he learned who he really was, and he "forsook Egypt, not fearing the wrath of the king."

I join with faithful parents everywhere in declaring that we know who we are, we understand our responsibilities as parents, and we do not fear the wrath of the prince of darkness. We trust in the light of the Lord.

Like Jochebed, we raise our families in a wicked and hostile world—a world as dangerous as the courts of Egypt ruled by Pharaoh. But, like Jochebed, we also weave around our children a protective basket—a vessel called "the family"—and guide them to safe places where our teachings can be reinforced in the home and at church.[6]

The basket Jochebed constructed was called an "ark" (see Exodus 2:3). This small craft carried Moses safely down troubled waters just as Noah's ark kept his family safe on the deadly rising flood. An ark is a type for families—like Noah's and Jochebed's—a shelter we can build for our children. Jochebed used bulrushes to weave the basket and slime and pitch to line the cracks. She made his shelter watertight. She left no openings, no cracks to allow water to seep in.

As parents, we should study and apply this metaphor to our lives. We can liken the story of Moses's journey down the Nile to our families, just as Moroni's fortifications are a symbol for our homes. Both an ark and an extensive barrier surrounding a city are tightly fitted to keep the enemy out. Family rituals and scheduled gatherings like daily mealtimes, family scripture study, prayers, church worship, visiting the needy, and doing chores together form tight bonds between family members.

We must ask ourselves: how active and committed are we in building a "place of retreat" or ark, made with peace and love and testimony? Even after Moroni's initial success, he continued his preparations knowing the enemy would return. Indeed, Satan will never be satisfied and will always be looking for "cracks." Try to visualize the ingenious architectural plans Moroni used that are described in chapter 50. As you read the following, pay attention to how many levels of defense he used.

The Nephites continued to dig up heaps of earth around the perimeter of the cities. Timbers were embedded on top of these ridges of earth (see Alma 50:1–2). The poles stood vertically, and on top of these he built a frame of pickets. Moroni caused towers to be erected on top of the pickets and "places of security to be built upon those towers" (Alma 50:4). The enemy's stones and arrows could not reach those places of security, but the Nephites could easily debilitate the advancing armies by launching weapons from above.

Why are all these details of fortress building in the book of Alma? They illustrate the extent to which a righteous parent should go to protect the walls of their home. Moroni layered strategy upon strategy—five layers of defense—to strengthen his fortress. We need to examine our homes and see where they are compromised and the enemy could expose and penetrate. Is there too much time spent on amusement at the expense of quality interactions and teaching? Does anger and contention allow the enemy to feed on a negative spirit? Do we neglect the greater matters because smaller distractions get in the way?

Captain Moroni did not wait until the enemy came knocking to take action; he scouted out their weaknesses and exploited them. He took the offensive rather than defensive approach in battle. "The people of the Nephites were *aware* of the intent of the Amlicites, and therefore they did *prepare* to meet them; yea, they did *arm themselves*" (Alma 2:12; emphasis added). What three things did they do? They became *aware* of the enemy's tactics, *prepared* accordingly, and *armed themselves* with all manner of weapons. Most importantly, Moroni did not rely solely on the arm of flesh. He sent men to the prophet to ascertain what the Lord would have him do (see Alma 43:23). We must likewise seek out the Lord's will in our lives.

Let us consider the potency of fortress building and wearing spiritual armor in these perilous times. I know many vigilant parents who take an offensive approach like Moroni. Many build strongholds when filtering and monitoring their children's activities on the computer and other electronic devices. They use a multilayered approach of anti-porn filters, software, strict usage rules, and personal vigilance to keep their children safe. When there are choices available, some parents take the offensive when selecting the right school for their children to attend. They scout out, gather information, and pray for answers. During the school year, they are vigilant in monitoring the activities in their child's classroom. Perhaps they volunteer at the school to be familiar with the environment or join a committee to be part of the process to make improvements in school policies and procedures. Principled parents create a welcoming home for their children's friends so they can assess their son's or daughter's social tendencies. Similarly, parents stay involved in their children's extracurricular activities, perhaps volunteering as mentors, coaches, or chaperones, or sitting on a board of directors. Most important, they talk to their children openly about these issues and listen to what their child is thinking. Thus, parents who are proactive and involved in their children's lives see firsthand what their children face, which gives them opportunities to shape the future.

Communities are only as strong as their families. Committed families can reach out and strengthen their communities. Collectively, we can be a force for great good. Likewise, the community as a whole as well as extended family, friends, and neighbors can strengthen a family in crisis. Elder M. Russell Ballard called us to this duty:

> In today's world, where Satan's aggression against the family is so prevalent, parents must do all they can to fortify and defend their families. But their efforts may not be enough. Our most basic institution of family desperately needs help and support from the extended family and the public institutions that surround us. Brothers and sisters, aunts and uncles, grandparents and cousins can make a powerful difference in the lives of children. Remember that the expression of love and encouragement from an extended family member will often provide the right influence and help a child at a critical time.[7]

What parents have done in previous generations may not be enough for our day. We cannot sit back anymore and hope all goes well. Elder L. Tom Perry warned, "Teaching in the home is becoming increasingly important in today's world, where the influence of the adversary is so widespread and he is attacking, attempting to erode and destroy the very foundation of our society, even the family. Parents must resolve that teaching in the home is a most sacred and important responsibility."[8]

When we arm our children, we prepare them to walk confidently out into the world, even among the "fiery darts of the adversary" and remain unharmed. My brother was taught by our goodly parents within the safety of our home. During one high school basketball season, his team went to a tournament in Las Vegas. The team members all gathered one night in my brother's hotel room and ordered pornographic videos and solicited a prostitute to their room. My brother had a decision to make. They told him to "be a man." However, protected by his virtue, covenants, and priesthood power, he fled the room, much like Joseph in Egypt. He found refuge (ironically) as a sixteen-year-old, walking the Strip alone in Vegas. Years later, he and his wife continue to teach the gospel to their own six faithful children.

Additional counsel was given on this theme by Elder Neil L. Anderson. We end with his inspired words: "We hold in our arms the rising generation. They come to this earth with important responsibilities and great spiritual capacities. We cannot be casual in how we prepare them. Our challenge as parents and teachers is not to create a spiritual core in their souls but rather to fan the flame of their spiritual core already aglow with the fire of their premortal faith."[9]

Parenting principles from Captain Moroni: Raise a familial standard and teach and live by its principles. We need to be aware, prepare, and arm ourselves in offense to Satan's attacks. Build a place of retreat, safety, and protection, as well as outfit ourselves and our children with the armor of God to protect ourselves against Satan's attacks.

NOTES

1. Henry B. Eyring, "The Power of Teaching Doctrine," *Ensign,* May 1999, 73.

2. M. Russell Ballard, "Filling the World with Goodness and Truth," *Ensign,* July 1996, 12.

3. "The Family: A Proclamation to the World," *Ensign,* November 1995, 102.

4. "The Living Christ: The Testimony of the Apostles," *Ensign,* April 2000, 3.

5. M. Russell Ballard, "What Matters Most Is What Lasts Longest," *Ensign*, November 2005, 41–42.

6. Robert D. Hales, "With All the Feelings of a Tender Parent: A Message of Hope to Families," *Ensign,* May 2004, 89.

7. M. Russell Ballard, "What Matters Most Is What Lasts Longest," *Ensign,* November 2005, 43.

8. L. Tom Perry, "Mothers Teaching in the Home," *Ensign,* May 2010, 30.

9. Neil L. Anderson, "Tell Me the Stories of Jesus," *Ensign*, May 2010, 108.

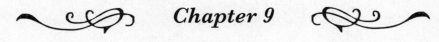

Chapter 9

CHRIST AND HIS DISCIPLES: THE POWER OF BELIEVING

No one knows our children better than we do (except our Heavenly Father, of course, who knows them infinitely better). We know their habits, unique personalities, talents, weaknesses, fears, and potential. Sometimes they live far below their privilege. A great disappointment in life can be knowing the gap between who our children are and what they could be. Nevertheless, our parenting practices will improve as we cultivate acceptance of others wherever they may be and have faith in whom they can become. One of life's sobering lessons is to appreciate, in small measure, the same feelings our Father in Heaven must feel about *us*.

Our exemplar in parenting, Jesus Christ, took ordinary men and turned them into extraordinary apostles and prophets. How did he do that? He founded parenting principles throughout his ministry. Let us begin with a life-altering event that occurred at the shores of the Sea of Galilee.

On this occasion, Simon Peter and his fishing partners, James and John, had toiled all night but caught no fish. Christ let them try and fail and exercise their best effort. It was not until morning, when the ships were docked and they were washing out their empty nets, that Jesus appeared and offered help. He told Peter to launch out his boat again, with the two of them inside. Peter explained their penury from the prior night's catch but cast out in spite of obvious misgivings. "And when they had this done, they inclosed a great multitude of fishes: and their net brake" (Luke 5:6).

Peter was astonished at this miracle. It was especially meaningful when he realized his own impressive wisdom and strength yielded nothing when compared to the Master who commanded the fish and the sea and all elements on earth. He fell down at Jesus's feet and cried, "Depart from me; for I am a sinful man, O Lord" (Luke 5:8). Indeed, he was sinful, as we all are. I doubt he was intentionally wicked; perhaps he was feeling somewhat the humility we will all experience when we approach Christ at the judgment bar. Our sinful nature, our nothingness before so great a deity, our unworthiness of so many blessings will be overwhelming!

Christ knew and accepted this man Peter—his shortcomings, his faults, his indiscretions—but more important, he saw his potential. He reassured him, "Fear not; from henceforth thou shalt catch men" (Luke 5:10) and selected him as one of the chosen few to become his chief Apostle. Christ did not dwell on Peter's weaknesses or sins; instead, he believed in him and brought out the best in Peter. He offered discipleship and lifted Peter to walk on higher ground. Christ used the "as if" principle. He saw Peter, along with the other disciplines, *as if* they were great men. They were not great yet, but Christ saw the best in them and acted as if they were already there. He did this patiently, very patiently!

Christ showed us that imperfect people are best built up. We can do the same with our children. When our son, Jared, was in second grade, he had a phenomenal teacher. At parent-teacher conferences, this teacher couldn't say enough praise about our son, and we could feel his genuine interest in Jared's potential. He summed up his honest admiration by exclaiming, "He's the next cure for cancer." Needless to say, that was a highlight year for our son.

Elder O. Vincent Haleck defined the attitude of seeing the best in ourselves as well as our children as having a "vision": "When we study the life of our Savior and His teachings, we see him amongst the people, teaching, praying, lifting, and healing. When we emulate Him and do the things we see Him do, we begin to see a vision of who we can become. . . . Just as the Savior saw great potential in his early disciples, He also sees the same in us."[1]

We need to be gentle with ourselves as well as our children when our weaknesses can be so glaring. There is no need to ruminate over faults like a pile of compost. There is no need to throw accusations in frustration such as, "Why don't you ever . . . ?" or "Why are you so . . . ?" *What we focus on will be what we get.* Another pitfall can be overstating or rehearsing *our* rightness in a condescending tone as the adult and *their* wrongness as the dependent: "You want to play? Have you done your homework yet? I don't *think* so!" or "How many times do I have to show you how to set the table? *It's not that hard!*" Parenting should not be about superiority, but instead, priority.

My sister experienced the negative impact of someone focusing on the deficits rather than the potential in our children. When her very bright and confident daughter, Janean, began fourth grade, she returned home each day saying, "I don't like school." Soon after, she began sighing, "I'm not good at math" or "I'm not good at reading."

At a parent-teacher conference in October, my sister got the distinct impression the teacher was talking unusually slow and "dumbing down" her words as if my sister had trouble understanding. During the conferences, the teacher kept pointing to a reading test score of 10 percent. She began talking about enrolling Janean in a remedial reading class. My sister was stunned. She explained to the teacher how her daughter had always been a top student in prior years. The conference ended in great discouragement.

That night, the teacher phoned my sister. She said in an apologetic voice, "I knew something had to be wrong. The score I received from the testing center the first week of school and what you said about her didn't make sense. So I called the teacher from last year. Her third grade teacher said Janean had been one of her top students. So I checked the original test scores, and saw they had left off a zero when they sent the score to me." What should have been a 100 percent became a 10 percent because of one missing digit. Since the fourth-grade teacher neglected to have Janean read to her personally, but relied on the test score, the teacher had judged Janean as a 10-percent student, my sister as a 10-percent mother, and had consigned them both to that rank in life. Fortunately, when the teacher's perception was amended, the rest of the year improved.

President Monson spoke in a recent priesthood session about seeing the good in another and believing in the better person they may become one day. These principles are significant as we serve in church callings, in the workplace, as well as in our sacred and eternal calling as parents. Referring to less-active and nonmembers, young and old, he said:

It is our responsibility to give them opportunities to live as they should. We can help them to overcome their shortcomings. We must develop the capacity to see men not as they are at present but as they may become when they receive testimonies of the gospel of Christ . . .

In one particular meeting, N. Eldon Tanner, who was then an Assistant to the Quorum of the Twelve, had just returned from his initial experience of presiding over the missions in Great Britain and western Europe. He told of a missionary who had been the most successful missionary whom he had met in all of the interviews he had conducted. He said that as he interviewed that missionary, he said to him, "I suppose that all of the people whom you baptized came into the Church by way of referrals."

The young man answered, "No, we found them all by tracting."

Brother Tanner asked him what was different about his approach— why he had such phenomenal success when others didn't. The young man said that he attempted to baptize every person whom he met. He said that if he knocked on the door and saw a man smoking a cigar and dressed in old clothes and seemingly uninterested in anything—particularly religion—the missionary would picture in his own mind what that man would look like under a different set of circumstances. In his mind he would look at him as clean-shaven and wearing a white shirt and white trousers. And the missionary could see himself leading that man into the waters of baptism. He said, "When I look at someone that way, I have the capacity to bear my testimony to him in a way that can touch his heart."[2]

I taught a young lady at Utah Valley University years ago with Down syndrome. She was a bright and cheerful student, very motivated to perform her best. I learned a little of her background during the semester. Her mother, along with another mother of a son with Down syndrome, attended a national convention for Down syndrome many years prior, when their children were young. Most parents were told in those days they would be lucky if their child could be taught to care for themselves. There was little prospect they could do much beyond that. The convention speaker asked the parents to imagine what their child could achieve in their lifetime. He told them to think high, to consider all possibilities. While they each silently thought—wished beyond hope—of what their child could achieve, he said, "Now I want you to double that."

My student's mother shared this story as we toured the facility she and the other mother founded after they returned from that convention.

There had been only one early intervention program for special needs children where they lived, and the program's philosophy was: "Love them, but don't expect much." Consequently, these two mothers resolved to begin a new center. They focused on the ability rather than the disability. Their facility now treats thousands of children and has helped thousands become more than previously realized. Because of these mothers' changed vision of what their children could be, their son and daughter have achieved much, much more than they ever would have imagined. The son with Down syndrome also attended the university, is a temple ordinance worker, and has been in over sixteen community theater productions. After his latest performance in *Fiddler on the Roof*, with a packed house every night, he came home and exclaimed, "Mom, it's such a burden to be famous!"

One of my children has had challenges expressing vulnerable emotions such as love, affection, sympathy, sorrow for wrongdoing, and sincere gratitude. As with us all, tender feelings are strengthened in safety, encouragement, and trust. Consequently, I applied the "as if" principle. I sometimes felt discouraged about rarely being appreciated over the years, yet I kindled a vision of that child *as if* they were able to express thankfulness or sorrow. No doubt it was difficult at times, but I trusted in that child's potential to develop those qualities. I treasured the other small ways they showed gratitude, even though it was not direct. I continued to outwardly express my thanks to this child *as if* they reciprocated. I imagined and hoped for the day when they be able to do so. Gradually, but very remarkably, it has come.

I use the "as if" principle in very small and practical ways on a regular basis. Squirmy kids in church? I whisper in their ear, "I sure appreciate your sitting so quietly so we can all hear the talks about Jesus." A child who is resistant to doing chores? "Thank you for mopping the floor anyway, even though you don't feel like it. You are awesome to be so helpful." A child spills food on the floor and walks away? My cheerful response: "Thank you for cleaning that up. I can see you were just going to get a rag to take care of the mess." More often than not, these not-so-willing children turn pliant under my encouraging hand. It's the power of believing!

It is important for us all to believe the best of others and ourselves. When our children make a mistake, we might hear them say in frustration, "I'm so stupid!" or "Why can't I do anything right?" (those phrases might be menacing inside our heads about our *own* mistakes). That is destructive, negative self-talk. We are what we think. Our thoughts dictate our words and actions. Repeated behaviors become our habits and our very natures. We should lift our thoughts, words, and actions to higher ground and offer our children a helping hand. A more appropriate reaction after a child's mistake is, "That's so unlike you. You are such a dependable/honest/kind person. I know you'll do better next time." I might joke with my teen by saying, "That was sure an aberration from your awesomeness!" Or, after a toddler's accidental fall, "Oops! Jump back up. You can do it!"

I once heard a story about a father whose son's friends took a joyride in a stolen car. They got into an accident and were punished by the authorities. When the father heard of the incident, he said to his son, "Oh, how tragic! I wish you would have been there with them. Then, none of that would have happened." Do you hear the confidence that father expressed in his son? How more likely will that son live up to his potential!

Christ also taught us by his example with the disciples to appreciate their uniqueness. He called Simon "the Rock," James and John "Sons of Thunder," and John "the Beloved." These monikers denote their nature—what Christ saw in them. Indeed, each was different, and Christ did not change what was their inherently true character. I am touched when I hear a parent call their child, "my love," "sweetheart," "buddy," or say, "Hey, beautiful!"

It should be of no surprise to discover we each learned a variety of "first lessons in the worlds of spirits" (D&C 138:56) before coming to earth to continue our secondary education. No doubt Mozart began his musical career way before birth; Galileo must have enrolled in advanced math, astronomy, and science classes in the pre-earth world. Often, as parents, we want our children to share our personal interests and excel where we excel. This can be realized in some cases. However, a father may have superior abilities and interest in sports but have a child who is uncoordinated with an aptitude for chess. A mother may love literature and music yet have a child who is tone deaf and prefers science. When our skillsets vary from our children's, it should not be a source of frustration, but a marvel of our different divine gifts we brought from the pre-earth life. We should recognize the special interests of our children (even when they are foreign to us!) and nurture them along as Christ did.

Some are born with certain limitations as part of the plan of salvation we chose to follow. Jesus taught us more about human nature than the nature of fishing when he called his disciples. It was Elder Neal A. Maxwell who said,

> The Lord, who was able to say to his disciples, "Cast the net on the right side of the ship" [John 21:6], knew beforehand that there was a multitude of fishes there. If he knew beforehand the movements and whereabouts of fishes in the little Sea of Tiberias, should it offend us that he knows beforehand which mortals will come into the gospel net? . . . There are clearly special cases of individuals with special limitations in life, which conditions we mortals cannot now fully fathom. For all we now know, the seeming limitations may have been an agreed-upon spur to achievement—a "thorn in the flesh" [2 Corinthians 12:7]. Like him who was "blind from birth," some come to bring glory to God [John 9:1–2]. We must be exceedingly careful about imputing either wrong causes or wrong rewards to all in such circumstances. They are in the Lord's hands, and he loves them perfectly. Indeed, some of those who have required much waiting upon in this life may be waited upon again by the rest of us in the next world—but for the highest of reasons![3]

For parents who are righteously raising children with special needs, these are comforting words. Each of us need to be more mindful of how we can appreciate the variances and tendencies in all children and support one another as parents of these beautiful spirit children of God. It is compassionate to remember that those who have disabled bodies, unique challenges, or limited abilities will have all things restored to them in the resurrection. "The soul shall be restored to the body, and the body to the soul; yea, and every limb and joint shall be restored to its body; yea, even a hair of the head shall not be lost; but all things shall be restored to their proper and perfect frame" (Alma 40:23).

Another grand episode that highlights the principle of potential occurred on the night of Christ's suffering and trial. Our Savior once again chose to overlook shortcomings of his disciples and see their possibilities. After the Last Supper, Christ pronounced that Peter would repeatedly waiver in his commitment to him. Jesus was well aware of Peter's faults ,but on the same night of his betrayal, he asked Peter to come to the olive garden to pray with him. He still showed confidence in him as his future prophet. Three times Christ left his unspeakable suffering in the Garden of Gethsemane to check on the three sleeping disciples. The first time he asked Peter, "What, could ye not watch with me one hour?" (Matthew

26:40). He encouraged them to watch and pray that they enter not into temptation. He saw their shortcomings (the flesh is weak) as a temptation common to all mortals. However, at the same time, he saw the good and recognized how their "spirit indeed is willing" (Matthew 26:41).

Imagine! During our Savior's greatest agony, his Atonement for the sins and shortcomings of all mankind, he left three times to watch over and encourage his beloved disciples—the same number of times that Peter would soon deny knowing the Christ. Nevertheless, in consequence of the belief Christ showed in Peter—the "Rock" upon which he would build his church—Peter became the unwaveringly faithful, obedient, and steadfast prophet of the early Christian church.

Parenting Principles from Christ: We need to see the potential in our children and believe in who they can become. Nurture the unique gifts each child possesses even when their interests and talents are different than ours. Show confidence even when they stumble and disappoint. Applying the "as if" principle can be a constructive exercise. By overlooking the weaknesses in our children and accepting them at whatever stage, we acknowledge our desire for the same treatment from our Father in Heaven.

NOTES

1. O. Vincent Haleck, "Having the Vision to Do," *Ensign,* May 2012, 102–3.

2. Thomas S. Monson, "See Others As They May Become," *Ensign,* November 2012, 69–70.

3. Neal A. Maxwell, "A More Determined Discipleship," *Ensign,* February 1979, 71–72.

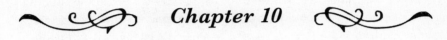

Chapter 10

HANNAH: THE POWER OF WAITING UPON THE LORD

Infertility was a distressing condition for those in ancient days. Having "seed" defined a couple and esteemed them by society. Moreover, bearing a son was critical for the continuation of the family line, for bestowal of inheritance, and for conformity to laws and customs that dictated the eldest son to care for his aging parents. Several biblical women were afflicted in the barren wilderness of infertility such as Hannah, Sarah, Rachel, and Elisabeth. We also read, as with Hannah, Sarah, and Rachel, that other mothers scorned and persecuted the barren woman, which only compounded their misery. According to biblical tradition, they believed the Lord was punishing them by shutting up their womb (see 1 Samuel 1:5–6).

Each of these women endured a test of faith and patience and were ultimately blessed with a child who was highly favored of the Lord. Hannah sought solace at the temple as she agonized over her infertility. She vowed a vow at this holiest place that if the Lord granted her a son, she would give him back to serve out his life in the temple. She was met by Eli, the high priest, who extracted the reason for her grieving. He showed compassion on her by declaring, "Go in peace: and the God of Israel grant thee thy petition that thou hast asked of him" (1 Samuel 1:17). Hannah, at last, bore a son and named him Samuel. She exulted in this private miracle and composed a passage of praise: "My heart rejoiceth in the Lord, mine horn is exalted in the Lord: my mouth is enlarged over mine enemies; because I rejoice in thy salvation" (1 Samuel 2:1). Truly, nothing is too hard for the Lord!

Consequently, Hannah enacted something almost unthinkable for a mother. After waiting so long and wading through so many afflictions, she gave her child up to the Lord for temple service. When the child was weaned (about two or three years old), she took Samuel to the temple and gave him to Eli to serve there. She remembered her vow and honored it. I've heard the joke among parents that if she would have waited until Samuel was a teenager, it wouldn't have been a sacrifice! I am always so touched by the tender anecdote of Hannah visiting her young son yearly thereafter and bringing a little coat she had made for him.

Hannah demonstrated a deep understanding that few parents appreciate. She said to Eli at the temple, "As thy soul liveth, my lord, I am the woman that stood by thee here, praying unto the Lord" (1 Samuel 1:26). She remembered how she grieved in that very place a few years earlier with a broken heart. Now, under quite opposite circumstances, her heart was overflowing with gratitude. She continued, "For this child I prayed; and the Lord hath given me my petition which I asked of him: Therefore also I have lent him to the Lord; as long as he liveth he shall be lent to the Lord" (1 Samuel 1:27–28).

What perspective on parenthood did she possess? She showed her gratitude in word *and* deed and kept her promise. Hannah used an interesting word twice: *lent*. Not only did she know all things in heaven and on earth are God's, she showed her appreciation accordingly. We are just stewards here on this earth. We are "tenders" of this garden, as was instructed to Adam. We are only passing through this second estate, and our children pass through us for a short time. They are borrowed from our Heavenly Father, and Hannah lent Samuel back in a supreme act of acknowledgement for His mercies. After all, He is the Father of our children's eternal spirits while we provide the mortal tabernacle for a time in which to dwell.

We are not asked to give up our children, nor are we expected to show our gratitude by such a sacrifice. However, we can allow the intent of Hannah's sacrifice to saturate our souls. First, as we raise children, we turn them over to our Heavenly Father as we seek to do His will in raising them. They were His first. He is in charge, and we must earnestly tether a partnership with Him. He knows them infinitely better than we do. Our job is to return them back to Him, having trained them in the way they should go (see Proverbs 22:6).

Second, the degree of Hannah's faith and obedience multiplied her blessings. Her life story could be an example from Elder Marion G. Romney's conference address, in which he quoted his mission president Elder Melvin J. Ballard: "A person cannot give a crust to the Lord without receiving a loaf in return."[1] Hannah may have given up her firstborn son, but in return, she received more children to raise. In 1 Samuel 2:21 we read, "And the Lord visited Hannah, so that she conceived, and bare three sons and two daughters. And the child Samuel grew before the Lord." What greater blessing could any parent desire! She was given six children—one with a holy calling and life's work dedicated to God.

Next, we understand that from an eternal reckoning of time, this earth life is just a glance of an eye. What makes anything lasting or meaningful are the sealing covenants we make at temple altars. As members of the restored Church, we make covenants with our Heavenly Father in the name of our Savior. We strive to rear children in righteousness to claim the sealing power of having an eternal family. Hannah may have given up her child temporarily, but she can claim him for eternity.

Hannah's offering to God echoed the sacrifice of Isaac by Abraham. "By faith Abraham, when he was tried, offered up Isaac: and he that had received the promises offered up his only begotten son" (Hebrews 11:17). After Abraham's trial, an angel appeared before the altar and declared that because Abraham had not withheld his son from the Lord, Abraham would be blessed with a multitude of posterity. His lineage would be so innumerable, they would be as the "stars of the heaven" and the "sand which is upon the sea shore" and be given power to subdue their enemies; through them, all the world would be blessed (see Genesis 22:15–18). Both Abraham and Hannah's sacrifices prefigured the eternal and everlasting one by our Heavenly Parent, who gave up His firstborn son so He could claim *all* His children.

Finally, all faithful Latter-day Saints who have had the blessing of children withheld from them during this short mortal probationary period are given promises under the Abrahamic covenant. If worthy, they will be given seed without number, and worlds without end. These blessings are bestowed unto the faithful who are sealed under the new and everlasting covenant.

Hannah exemplifies a faithful woman who waited upon the Lord and eventually had a multiplicity of posterity. We can all wait upon the Lord to receive promised blessings on His timetable—either in this life or the next. "What, then, does it mean to wait upon the Lord?" asked Elder Robert D. Hales. "In the scriptures, the word *wait* means to hope, to anticipate, and to trust. To hope and trust in the Lord requires faith, patience, humility, meekness, long-suffering, keeping the commandments, and enduring to the end."[2]

A dear friend of mine has been unable to conceive during mortality. She is an outstanding woman, capable in every way, including the gifts of mothering. Her perspective adds authenticity to the eternal truth of parenting and waiting upon our Father's infinite plan:

I distinctly remember a day during my senior year in high school when I was sitting in my guidance counselor's office and listening to her review my test scores, grades and scholarship opportunities. She made the comment that with my abilities and determination I could be a doctor, lawyer, professor—anything I wanted to be. My response to her was instant and definite, "Those are all great options, but to be honest, what I really want to be is a mother." It was true. I truly desired to raise a righteous posterity unto the Lord.

A number of years after that day in the counselor's office, I was sealed for time and eternity to my best friend and we embarked upon life's journey together with shared dreams of a large, happy family. Over a decade later, we were emotionally and financially spent, having done everything in our power to conceive children of our own and never having that dream realized. We had fasted, prayed and received priesthood blessings. We had done everything we knew how to do and there were times when I actually questioned if Heavenly Father didn't trust me enough to be a parent, that I wasn't good enough, that my faith was insufficient, or that I was being punished in some way that I didn't understand. Logically I knew this wasn't so, but these were thoughts from the adversary that I literally had to cast out in order to maintain hope and not become mired in self-pity.

As members of the Church, we belong to a culture that is, rightfully, completely family-oriented. LDS families tend to be larger than nonmember families, and our highest goals for eternal life involve continued offspring and family life. These eternal goals greatly impact the value we place on having families here on earth. It is very easy to begin to define oneself and one's partnership by the lack of the desired family, instead of by all the other amazing and wonderful aspects of a couple's shared life. It requires great care to continue to nurture one's partnership, to not place blame and to hold tight to one another rather than drift apart on the sea of unrealized expectations.

Eventually, after all the fruitless effort, my husband and I had to come to a place where we either had to accept the Lord's will for our lives or continue to "kick against the pricks." We decided to give up the desired pregnancy in order to pursue parenting in whatever form the Lord provided. We realized that conceiving and bearing a biological child does not a parent make. Love, unselfishness and a desire to bless a child's life are the most important elements of parenting—and these do not require a shared genetic code. In our case, we were able to find parenting joy through prayerful adoption; others find it through service careers that bless the lives of children, through volunteering in their church and community, as well as through sweet extended family and friend relationships. Every couple is different; every decision is personal and intensely private. Ward and family members need to be sensitive and trust that those who do not have children or large families have, in most cases, been extremely prayerful and diligent—that "in the quiet heart is hidden, sorrow that the eye can't see."

There will be difficult days, of course. I have to determinedly subdue my envy when medical procedures that failed for us inexplicably work for others. I shed tears each December as I look at friends' Christmas cards and the pictures of their beautiful families gracing our wall. Many Mother's Days at church were difficult. Baby showers and lengthy pregnancy and delivery stories are not my favorite things—I can't relate to this life experience that is such a common denominator for many women within my circle. Adoption is not a cure-all for infertility and brings its own challenges. Grief will be triggered in unique ways for every person struggling with a "family picture" that is different than the one they had hoped for and imagined.

The greatest gifts a person can give to those struggling with infertility are compassion and lack of judgment. Those of us experiencing infertility must also exercise that same compassion and lack of judgment for others when they make well-meaning but hurtful comments. We must exercise that same compassion and lack of judgment for ourselves. We can wallow in disappointment and define ourselves by our lack or we can choose to accept and make the most of what we have been given. We can center our lives in Christ by feasting on the scriptures, praying diligently, renewing our covenants and enduring patiently. As our faith grows, we can trust in the promises given by prophets through the ages that all things denied His righteous children during mortality will be restored in full in the life hereafter. My husband and I trust in those promises and they motivate us, comfort us (most of the time), and give meaning to our lives. For me personally, what I have come to know is that I am the one who must decide daily how I'll allow this challenge to shape my life and impact those I love.

Parenthood, no matter when it happens for us on the eternal continuum, is a divine and foreordained calling. Our first earthly mother received the name "Eve" because "she was the mother of all living" (Moses 4:26). Adam pronounced this while they were still in the garden, childless. In other words, he acknowledged her eternal nature as a nurturer long before she even bore a child. Therefore, all righteous couples will have an opportunity to bear and rear children at some point in the plan of salvation. We are all "parents" whether or not we presently have children. This plan is also called the "great plan of happiness" (Alma 42:8), and parenting is part of that happy plan! Our test on earth is to learn the divine attributes God has as a Heavenly Parent and earnestly align our nature to His.

In sum, Elder Richard G. Scott offered this promise: "Some of you may feel lonely and unappreciated and cannot see how it will be possible for you to have the blessings of marriage and children or your own family. All things are possible to the Lord, and He keeps the promises He inspires His prophets to declare. Eternity is a long time. Have faith in those promises and live to be worthy of them so that in His time the Lord can make them come true in your life. With certainty, you will receive every promised blessing for which you are worthy."[3]

Parenting principles from Hannah: *Nothing is too hard for the Lord.* If we trust His mercy and power and the promises in our temple covenants, no blessing of offspring will be withheld from us in the eternities. Whatever sacrifice we make in bearing and rearing righteous children will return to us in an abundance of blessings. Finally, rearing children should be a partnership with God. He knows our children better than we, and His will should inform all our childrearing practices.

NOTES

1. Marion G. Romney, "Welfare Services: The Savior's Program," *Ensign,* November 1980, 93.

2. Robert D. Hales, "Waiting upon the Lord: Thy Will Be Done," *Ensign,* November 2011, 72.

3. Richard G. Scott, "The Eternal Blessings of Marriage," *Ensign,* May 2011, 97.

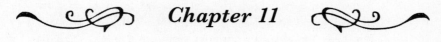

Chapter 11

JACOB AND ENOS: THE POWER OF CONSISTENCY

Repetition is the mother of all learning. The gospel plan must be taught and retaught under different conditions and at different stages in our children's development. Lessons are planted, nourished, and tended—all of which require time and vigilance. The five wise virgins prepared their lamps one drop of oil at a time (see Matthew 25:1–13). In short, we cannot rush a testimony or expect a child to get it right the first time.

Jacob's family in the Book of Mormon is an excellent case study of paternal diligence and a child's eventual response. Jacob did not record the details of family home evenings and fireside chats, but we can be certain there were many. Enos described his father Jacob as a "just man—for he taught me in the language, and also in the nurture and admonition of the Lord—and blessed be the name of my God for it" (Enos 1:1). Jacob taught his children, drop by drop, the truths of the gospel until the mysteries of the kingdom became "a well of living water, springing up unto eternal life" (D&C 63:23). These small but steady acts eventually carved a fertile channel where his son could sink deep roots.

Enos recorded that as he was out hunting one day, the "words which I had *often* heard my father speak concerning eternal life, and the joy of the saints, sunk deep into my heart. And my soul hungered; and I kneeled down before my Maker, and I cried unto him in mighty prayer and supplication for mine own soul; and all the day long did I cry unto him; yea, and when the night came I did still raise my voice high that it reached the heavens" (Enos 1:4; emphasis added). Enos yearned to be relieved of his sinful burdens, and he was forgiven and blessed by the Lord.

> We don't know the nature or extent of Enos's sins, but it could have been that earlier lessons from his father Jacob were not appreciated. Elder Henry B. Eyring assured, The years pass, we teach the doctrine the best we can, and yet some still do not respond. There is sorrow in that. But there is hope in the scriptural record of families. Think of Alma the Younger and Enos. In their moments of crisis, they remembered the words of their fathers, words of the doctrine of Jesus Christ. It saved them. Your teaching of that sacred doctrine will be remembered.[1]

It is tempting to abandon our parenting responsibilities when children do not reciprocate our efforts. In an address to the women in the church, Elder M. Russell Ballard declared,

> Now, mothers, I understand that it sometimes appears that our children aren't paying attention to the lessons we're trying to teach them. Believe me—I've seen that glazed-over look that comes to the eyes of teenagers just when you're coming to what you think is the best part of your instruction. Let me assure you that even when you think your daughter is not listening to a thing you say, she is still learning from you as she watches you to see if your actions match your words.[2]

Think of a candle. How many times does it take to hand dip a wick before a candle immerges from the wax? Many, many times! A standard candle wears at least two hundred coats of wax. A larger candle can easily have many more in order to hold a substantial flame. The process takes time and patience; between each coat, the developing candle needs to cool and dry. By way of comparison, we often find an interesting scriptural expression of a people or individual who "wax strong" in becoming good or evil. "Waxing" is a slow process that describes a person who habitually immerses in daily choices that ultimately determine their character. There is a lesson in this for parents. Day by day, our unfailing efforts can create children who are strong enough to hold light.

The following scenario may occur in a typical LDS home: diligent parents invite their children to family scripture study, the dinner table, or family home evenings. Most children come (especially if they are in the formative years), but one may disappear, or two . . . under a blanket, into a bedroom, or simply into thin air. Instead of becoming discouraged and giving up, we must keep going. Hold scripture study at the foot of a bed with a "sleeping" teenager or within earshot, but hold it anyway. If they have a cell phone, text your child a short summary of what you studied and tell them you missed them and love them! Invite them to come the next time. Be creative and follow the Spirit. The act of simply opening the pages of the Book of Mormon and reading the words aloud in our homes invites the Spirit to permeate bedroom walls and invisible barriers. There is power in the word; it reaches from one room to the next, from one heart to another. Elder Marion G. Romney made this life-altering promise:

> I feel certain that if, in our homes, parents will read from the Book of Mormon prayerfully and regularly, both by themselves and with their children, the spirit of that great book will come to permeate our homes and all who dwell therein. The spirit of reverence will increase; mutual respect and consideration for each other will grow. The spirit of contention will depart. Parents will counsel their children in greater love and wisdom. Children will be more responsive and submissive to the counsel of their parents. Righteousness will increase. Faith, hope, and charity—the pure love of Christ—will abound in our homes and lives, bringing in their wake peace, joy, and happiness.[3]

This promised blessing has been realized in countless homes. Are you one who needs to exercise faith and obedience by reading that book more frequently? Again, the integrity of our actions and instructions year after year *will* make an impression on our children.

Moses knew about weaving the Savior and his commandments into every moment of life. He received two stone tablets on the mount from Jehovah and warned the Israelites to continuously keep the law in front of them. They were to learn the statutes and commandments and teach them to their children. "And thou shalt teach them diligently unto thy children, and shalt talk of them when thou sittest in thine house, and when thou walkest by the way, and when thou liest down, and when thou risest up" (Deuteronomy 6:7); in other words, in all places and at all times.

In order to lay these words up in their hearts and minds, Moses commanded the Israelites to write the law on strips of paper that were tied to their foreheads and hands in the form of phylacteries and to set them inside doorposts. They took his directive very literally! Wherever they cast their eyes, they saw God's word in some form.

We can apply the spiritual aspect of this commandment. Whatever we say with our lips or hold in our hands—to read or to decorate our homes—should reflect virtue and a love of God. What do our children see in our homes as they look around? What do they hear? What are some visible objects that remind you and them of the Lord? We should have the scriptures, Church materials, and other print as well as gospel art surrounding us. Our leaders have counseled us to fill our homes with uplifting music and to adorn our walls with pictures of the Savior and the temple and other sacred art. One day, a child who was not raised by parents who practiced LDS beliefs or lifestyles visited my home. He scanned the living room and remarked, "You sure got a lot of Jesus around here."

We might have images of Jesus and scriptures around us, but what matters more is that we refer often to them. Just as we feed our physical bodies each day, we feed our spirits when we open up books of scripture, read them with real intent, and teach and testify to our children whenever appropriate. Nephi stated how Christ should be an integral and natural part of family life: "We talk of Christ, we rejoice in Christ, we preach of Christ, we prophesy of Christ, and we write according to our prophecies, that our children may know to what source they may look for a remission of their sins" (2 Nephi 25:26). Surely this requires repetition! Elder Holland expounded on this Book of Mormon prophet's words:

> Nephi-like, might we ask ourselves what our children know? From us? Personally? Do our children know that we love the scriptures? Do they see us reading them and marking them and clinging to them in daily life? Have our children ever unexpectedly opened a closed door and found us on our knees in prayer? Have they heard us not only pray *with* them but also pray *for* them out of nothing more than sheer parental love? Do our children know we believe in fasting as something more than an obligatory first-Sunday-of-the-month hardship? Do they know that we have fasted for them and for their future on days about which they knew nothing? Do they know we love being in the temple, not least because it provides a bond to them that neither death nor the legions of hell can break?[4]

Adam and Eve, our first parents, knew their solemn responsibilities and both "blessed the name of God, and *they made all things known* unto their sons and their daughters" (Moses 5:12; emphasis added). Surely that took many years and diligent effort. Elder L. Tom Perry specified,

> Parents must bring light and truth into their homes by one family prayer, one scripture study session, one family home evening, one book read aloud, one song, and one family meal at a time. They know that

the influence of righteous, conscientious, persistent, daily parenting is among the most powerful and sustaining forces for good in the world. The health of any society, the happiness of its people, their prosperity, and their peace all find common roots in the teaching of children in the home.[5]

When our oldest son was a toddler, I began playing the church's audio recordings of the children's scripture stories each night when he went to bed. He listened to those night and night, year after year, until he was a teenager. He gained a love and incredible knowledge of the scriptures that remains with him to this day.

We taught our youngest daughter the principle of tithing for a few years before she actually earned a dollar on which to pay tithing. When the day came for her to pay her 10 percent, all prior lessons were not nearly as meaningful as that one Sunday where she felt the acute sacrifice of giving up her first dime to the Lord. She paused for a moment and looked at me with eyes that wanted to believe. It was hard! Over the years, she has exercised this faithful muscle and now pays tithing easily and obediently. Another daughter had a financial blessing recently, and I remarked, "You have been paying your tithing so consistently your entire life that Heavenly Father just opened the window today and poured out a blessing when you needed it." I was able to use all the prior acts of obedience as a reference to which the blessing was predicated (see D&C 130:20–21).

We will not always be present when our children are tested. We have just a few short years (moments really, in reflection) to raise our children from embryo to exaltation. If we have nourished their faith and testimony with consistent and loving lessons over the years, they will be more equipped to stand on their own. They will be able to fight their own battles, like the two thousand young warriors who were taught to be obedient and did *"remember the words . . .* that their mothers had taught them"* (Alma 57:21; emphasis added). That is what the Ammonite mothers found when all their sons returned home safely from battle. They are likely to hunger and thirst after righteousness. That is what Jacob discovered when his son Enos came home from hunting one day.

Parenting principles from Jacob and Enos: We must consistently and explicitly teach the truths that we know. Our children must see us studying and sharing personal insights from the scriptures and other church material so it is a part of their everyday life. We need to repeat the teachings of the gospel many times and in many different situations. Our homes should reflect Christian virtues by all we see and hear.

NOTES

1.   Henry B. Eyring, "The Power of Teaching Doctrine," *Ensign,* May 1999, 74.

2.   M. Russell Ballard, "Mothers and Daughters," *Ensign*, May 2010, 20.

3.   Marion G. Romney, "The Book of Mormon," *Ensign,* May 1980, 67.

4.   Jeffrey R. Holland, "A Prayer for the Children," *Ensign,* May 2003, 87.

5.   L. Tom Perry, "Mothers Teaching Children in the Home," *Ensign,* May 2010, 30.

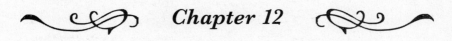

Chapter 12

CHRIST AND THE NEPHITES: THE POWER OF BEHOLDING

There are many symbols tied to the sacrament. One we might fail to notice is the value of the individual. By the very act of internalizing the emblems of Christ's sacrifice, one by one, we affirm His love for us personally. We do not administer and receive ordinances en masse; on the contrary, we accept them one by one. Since it is true of all ordinances, it is also the ideal of teaching the gospel—to one person at a time. Even when teaching a group in Primary or children of various ages in a family home evening lesson, children learn most effectively when they are personally engaged, participating, and applying the truths of the gospel to their own lives. Hence, parents who are effective teachers will individualize the needs of each child. They will regard each child as Christ did during his ministry.

After Christ's crucifixion and burial in Jerusalem, he appeared as a resurrected being to the Nephites on the American continent. Faithful saints had been awaiting his coming as the prophets had foretold. They met the resurrected Lord at the temple grounds in the city Bountiful. Christ invited them to come forward and feel the prints of the nails in his hands and feet and wound in his side as a witness he suffered and died for them. "And it came to pass that the multitude went forth, and thrust their hands into his side, and did feel the prints of the nails in his hands and in his feet; and this they did do, going forth *one by one* until they had all gone forth, and did see with their eyes and did feel with their hands, and did know of a surety and did bear record, that it was he of whom it was written by the prophets, that should come" (3 Nephi 11:15; emphasis added).

I am struck by all the detailed, individual witnesses that are recounted in this event. Notice the many ways each person *beheld* the resurrected Lord. They *thrust their hands into his side*, they *felt the prints* of nails by *touching his hands and feet*, they *saw with their eyes* and *felt with their hands* and then *bore record* (testifying to others, listening to each other's witness, as well and writing down their testimonies). They virtually used all their physical capacity to take in and bear record of that sacred event. In a similar symbolic witness, we "take in" the sacramental tokens of Christ's Atonement, and on fast Sunday, we bear record of His sacrifice. Keep this in mind as we discuss the power of beholding.

Subsequently, Christ showed compassion on the sick and afflicted and healed each one. He then commanded the children be brought to him. "And he took their little children, *one by one*, and blessed them, and prayed unto the Father for them. And when he had done this he wept again; and he spake unto the multitude, and said unto them: *Behold your little ones*" (3 Nephi 17:21; emphasis added).

Behold carries a bold admonition for parents. To "behold," we must stop and pay attention to *each child*. Elder M. Russell Ballard observed, "Notice that He didn't say 'glance at them' or 'casually observe them' or 'occasionally take a look in their general direction.' He said to *behold* them. To me that means that we should embrace them with our eyes and with our hearts; we should see and appreciate them for who they really are: spirit children of our Heavenly Father, with divine attributes."[1] Beholding takes time, love, and respect. It connotes seeing a child inside and out. *It involves all our senses*. The question arises: How can parents truly behold their children? The account of Christ's ministry to the Nephite people, among other subsequent applications from the scriptures, addresses this principle.

After the resurrected Lord proclaimed his ministry and Atonement to the Nephites, called the Twelve, and taught the doctrine of His church, and after the multitude felt the tokens in his hands and feet, Christ told them, "My time is at hand" (3 Nephi 17:1). In other words, their meeting had ended. He dismissed them to return home, ponder and pray, and prepare themselves for his next visit. Christ even specified what he was to do next: "But now I go unto the Father, and also to show myself unto the lost tribes of Israel" (v. 4). The Savior had a divine assignment to complete elsewhere. It is of great significance what happened next. "And it came to pass that when Jesus had thus spoken, he cast his eyes round about again on the multitude, and beheld they were in tears, and did look steadfastly upon him as if they would ask him to tarry a little longer with them" (v. 5).

The next word from our Savior was "Behold." Christ put aside his personal demands to behold the present needs of those of his ministry. I delight in the fact that he was never about schedules but about people. Following his example, again we learn how to understand, appreciate, and respond to the needs of others. He continued, "My bowels are filled with compassion towards you" (3 Nephi 17:6). We can likewise be filled with compassion by casting our eyes upon our children more often, discerning their hearts. Like the Nephites, our children may not verbalize their actual needs or desires. Jesus knew they wanted him to stay longer by looking into their eyes and seeing into their hearts. He had no other agenda in mind. He declared, "I perceive that ye desire . . ." and stayed a while longer on that significant day. What are your child's desires?

I was once interviewed for a temple recommend where a member of the stake presidency (whom I had never met) took extra time to "behold" me. He began many statements with "I perceive that . . ." and followed with many insights he could not have known without the spirit of discernment. He knew my desires. He recognized my potential. He affirmed my goodness. It was one of the most spiritual experiences of my life. I was enlivened by the Spirit as I left his office and could never adequately describe the pure light and power I felt for days after.

The first-day meeting between Christ and the Nephites was extended because Christ perceived their needs and responded accordingly. He healed all those who were brought to Him. We too can heal hearts when we stop to know and understand the hurts our children are suffering. Here is the certainty: If Christ had not stopped, felt, and responded to the Nephites' needs, think of what they would have missed! They would not have been healed, heard Christ's sublime prayer, felt inconceivable joy, witnessed Christ weep in their behalf and bless their children individually, or experienced the unspeakable sight of cloven heavens with angels descending and administering to their children, encircled by fire (see vv. 21–25). We must consider what blessings we, as well as our children, are missing if we do not stop, put aside our agendas, and behold them.

Jesse, a patriarch in the Old Testament, learned how to behold his sons; he learned to see them as God sees them. Samuel the prophet came to Jesse's house to choose the next king. Jesse brought his sons before the prophet . . . the ones he thought were worthy of such a calling. Samuel beheld Jesse's seven sons as they passed before them, one by one, but none were selected. The Spirit restrained Samuel from choosing any of them. The Lord instructed Samuel, "Look not on his countenance, or on the height of his stature; because I have refused him: for the Lord seeth not as man seeth; for man looketh on the outward appearance, but the Lord looketh on the heart" (1 Samuel 16:7).

Consequently, Samuel inquired if all the sons were present. David, the one son Jesse had not considered, was out tending sheep. Jesse had dismissed this child from the selection process, passing his own judgment upon him. Jesse had not beheld David from the inside out, using God's eyes. At Samuel's request, he called David from the fields. As soon as David, the shepherd boy, entered, the Lord said to Samuel, "Arise, anoint him: for this is he" (v. 12).

Joseph Smith Sr. and Lucy Mack Smith were outstanding parents in looking "on the heart." They raised a faithful, humble son who became the prophet of the last dispensation. In their family's initial quest to find a church to join, the parents exposed their children to the religious sects of the day, allowing them to choose the one they felt was right. Joseph Jr., however, reflected during a long period about their creeds and deeds and read continually from the Bible to find answers to his sobering decision.

Joseph finally concluded to seek divine guidance, and in response to prayer, he received a visitation from God the Father and His Son, Jesus Christ. While conversing about his questions and concerns, Joseph discovered his Father had a special calling for him to restore the true Church upon the earth. Afterward, he returned home and was so overcome by the experience of a theophany, his strength faltered. He wrote, "And as I leaned up to the fireplace, mother inquired what the matter was" (JSH 1:20).

It was a small thing, to lean against a fireplace. However, Lucy Smith beheld her child Joseph at a subtle yet critical moment in his life. She had many other children to capture her attention and surely had plenty of work to do, as women did in that time and circumstance, but she stopped to pay attention to one son leaning against the fireplace. She knew his manner well enough and had observed him in such a variety of conditions that she knew something had changed. His reply to her concern was typical of a teenager, "Never mind, all is well—I am well enough off," but confided, "I have learned for myself that Presbyterianism is not true" (JSH 1:20). By noticing her child at that moment and at subsequently decisive periods, she became one of the first of the family to be converted to the message of the restored gospel.

We could additionally draw a favorable conclusion about Joseph's righteous father. After the angel Moroni's third visit to Joseph within a few hours, Joseph was again stripped of strength. He tried to resume his usual manual labor the next morning but was unable. His father could have been consumed with his own work and worries, but he stopped to notice his ailing son. Father Smith sent his son home to rest, whereupon Joseph witnessed a fourth visit from the same angel. Moroni instructed Joseph to return to his father in the fields and tell him what had happened. He did as he was commanded. As a result of Joseph's father beholding his son and responding to his needs, he heard first of the heavenly message and affirmed, "It was of God" (JSH 1:50).

Do we frequently stop and behold our children, seeing them through God's eyes? Do we look with awe at their uniqueness, beauty, curiosity and innocence? Do we treasure the brief time each child spends under our care? Do we, like the Nephites and Christ, use all our physical capacity to understand and form a relationship with them? Do we stop whenever possible to behold their play or inquisitive faces? Or are we too busy beholding our electronic handheld devices and computer screens? I treasure all my children and especially appreciate the fleeting moments with my youngest that represented finality to my mortal parenting. After beholding so many of his precious preschool milestones, I wrote about him:

My Creations
To Daniel

I wonder at the cosmos,
my next handiwork—
a star or two,
after I'm through
and graduated
to Godhood.

In your bright,
five-year-old eyes,

I see Saturn's rings,
the blaze of things
pulsing the heavens,
spinning into orbit.

I created your
passionate perfection—
fingers learning math,
a bursting laugh,
legs churning
a two-wheeled bike.

After you, how easy
will be a veined leaf, mountain peak,
a grain of sand—
holding the sea in one hand,
sowing stars in outer furrows
while I stride the planets.

Parents can send a strong message that they care about "the one" when they take time with each child, doing what that child loves. Legos and action figures do not naturally captivate my attention, but over the years, I have become quite proficient at building a decent airplane and reenacting battles with plastic army men with my sons. Elder Robert D. Hales voiced his concern on this issue. Take note of all the senses he mentions as we take time to behold:

Similarly, mothers and fathers, as you drive or walk children to school or their various activities, do you use the time to talk with them about their hopes and dreams and fears and joys? Do you take the time to have them take the earplugs from their MP3 players and all the other devices so that they can hear you and feel of your love? The more I live, the more I recognize that the teaching moments in my youth, especially those provided by my parents, have shaped my life and made me who I am.

It is impossible to overestimate the influence of parents who understand the hearts of their children. Research shows that during the most important transitions of life—including those periods when youth are most likely to drift away from the Church—the greatest influence does not come from an interview with the bishop or some other leader but from the regular, warm, friendly, caring interaction with parents.[2]

I admire parents who frequently take their children, one-on-one, on a date. I love to see a parent and child sharing a laugh or inside joke together. We have a tradition that when my husband and I travel together, we take a child with us. These have been incredible bonding experiences. Even the simplest bedtime rituals can be significantly personal. When tucking my youngest in, I like to ask, "How much do I love you?" and he always responds, "All the way to heaven." Married or single parents can spend time reflecting on a particular child each week. As they discuss and concentrate their prayers about a single child weekly, that focus—that "beholding" of a child—will allow the Spirit to inspire them how to uplift, teach, and detect potential problems.

Early warnings come when we spend quality time with a child, one-on-one, in order to perceive potential problems. Elder David A. Bednar taught three components that will help us detect concerns early on in a child's development. He admonished,

> This early warning system applies to children of all ages and contains three basic components: (1) reading and talking about the Book of Mormon with your children, (2) bearing testimony of gospel truths spontaneously with your children, and (3) inviting children as gospel learners to act and not merely be acted upon. Parents who do these things faithfully will be blessed to recognize early signals of spiritual growth in or challenges with their children and be better prepared to receive inspiration to strengthen and help those children.[3]

One-on-one scenarios do not always present themselves easily, especially when there are multiple or mixed-age children in the home. It takes planning, effort, and, sometimes, creativity. A mother might volunteer to be the carpool chauffeur to overhear what her daughter and friends are discussing in the backseat and to have some together time alone in the car as well. A father might invite his son to pass him the tools as he works on the car, allowing time to chat informally. A parent returning from work could grab a baseball mitt and throw the ball with his son for a few minutes before dinner. A mother can assign each child a different night of the week to help her prepare the dinner so they can talk as they work side by side. I have found that my children suddenly open up while helping in the kitchen when they usually are reluctant to share their day with me. These informal but intentional settings should be individualized to the interests of each child.

Parents can easily spend one-on-one time each month as they carry out parent-child interviews. Elder Larry R. Lawrence suggested, "One of the most effective ways we can influence our sons and daughters is to counsel with them in private interviews. By listening closely, we can discover the desires of their hearts, help them set righteous goals, and also share with them the spiritual impressions that we have received about them. Counseling requires courage."[4]

Consistency is key. In our family, our children expect to be interviewed every fast Sunday. These can begin and end with prayer and the parent asking open-ended questions such as:

- What can I do to be a better parent?

- What were the happiest/saddest times this past week/month?

- Tell me about your personal scripture study and prayers.

- How do you feel about being a member of our family?

- Describe your friends/teachers/classes at school.

- What goals can we work on together?

As parents carry out this monthly meeting, children will come to count on their parents valuing their worth. If a child is resistant to a formal setting, find what is more appealing. Some teenagers might enjoy taking a walk, shopping, playing a game, or driving with their parent and would converse more readily in a more casual situation.

Our friends found how important flexibility and creativity are during interviewing. They bought a new house, and the master bathroom was designed with a large Jacuzzi bathtub. The parents prohibited the children from using their nice, private bathtub. When interviews came around one month, their dad told the children they could be interviewed anywhere they wanted. "Anywhere?" one son asked incredulously. After the dad confirmed his promise, this son announced he wanted to meet in the bathtub. The father and son sat in the empty tub and conducted their parent-child interview.

Father's blessings, patriarchal blessings, and other priesthood blessings are unique opportunities to pierce the veil and give a child the knowledge of who he or she is in the eyes of their Father in Heaven. Alma the Younger understood and lived this principle, as did other patriarchs in the scriptures. As they neared the close of their lives, these faithful men gave father's blessings, taught doctrine one-on-one, and discharged responsibilities to each child. When recorded in scripture, we can read the individual blessings and counsel tailored to the needs of each child.

Let us examine an excerpt from Alma's final interview with his son Helaman:

Alma: Believest thou the words which I spake unto thee concerning those records which have been kept?

Helaman: Yea, I believe.

Alma: Believest thou in Jesus Christ, who shall come?

Helaman: Yea, I believe all the words which thou hast spoken.

Alma: Will ye keep my commandments?

Helaman: Yea, I will keep thy commandments with all my heart.

Alma: Blessed art thou; and the Lord shall prosper thee in this land.

Alma's parent-child interview reaffirmed Helaman's worthiness before entrusting him with a private prophecy of the destruction of the Nephite nation (see Alma 45).

On an earlier date, Alma gathered his three sons, Helaman, Shiblon, and Corianton, to instruct them concerning their missions. His admonitions were as different as each son. We read, "Therefore, he caused that his sons should be gathered together, that he might give unto them *every one* his charge, *separately*, concerning the things pertaining unto righteousness" (Alma 35:16; emphasis added). The doctrine taught and the sensitivity to their level of understanding is noteworthy.

In the middle of his parent-child counsel, Alma said to Corianton, "And now, my son, *I perceive* there is somewhat more which doth worry your mind, which ye cannot understand. . . . Now behold, my son, I will explain this thing unto thee" (Alma 42:1–2l; emphasis added). This last son, Corianton, struggled with obedience and understanding. Alma perceived what he needed and elaborated his teaching to him. In the book of Alma, chapters 39–42 cover the foundational doctrine of the gospel that Alma teaches to Corianton: immorality is a sin, Christ's Atonement is infinite and eternal, the Fall and probationary period of mortality, the reality of the resurrection, the state of the righteous and wicked after death, and the mercy and justice of God. He briefly reflects on Corianton's wrong behavior but heavily teaches truth. The doctrine taught to

Corianton is by far the longest of all three sons because this son needed more intervention, like Christ extending his time with the Nephites.

The ideal learning environment was outlined by the Master Teacher: "Appoint among yourselves a teacher, and let not all be spokesmen at once; but let one speak at a time and let all listen unto his sayings, that when all have spoken that all may be edified of all, and that every man [and child] may have an equal privilege" (D&C 88:122). The main principles we gain from this scripture are that each person should have the opportunity to speak and be in charge as well as listen and be edified by others.

Beholding our children comes naturally in family councils and family home evenings. These are face-to-face settings for practicing the principles outlined in Doctrine and Covenants. We can foster skills of listening and respecting others. Every child should have a personal responsibility and a voice that is heard. In doing so, we value the "one." Elder Robert D. Hales counseled parents and leaders in the April 2010 general conference:

> When we have a family home evening, a family council, or a meaning-ful gospel conversation with our children, we have the opportunity to look into their eyes and tell them that we love them and that Heav-enly Father loves them. In these sacred settings, we can also help them understand, deep in their hearts, who they are and how fortunate they are to have come to this earth and to our home and to participate in the covenants we have taken in the temple to be a family forever.[5]

Family home evening offers many activities that even young children can carry out once a week. The number, ability, and ages of children can dictate how many responsibilities are given to each. Younger children can do most of them, albeit with assistance from an older sibling or parent. Some examples are as follows:

- Give the opening or closing prayer
- Choose and/or lead the closing or opening song
- Hand out papers/scriptures
- Hold a picture or visual aid
- Write down family planning/calendaring items
- Recite and comment on an Article of Faith or standard from *For the Strength of Youth* or *My Gospel Standards*
- Prepare and give the lesson

- Read a scripture or tell a scripture story

- Share a talent or achievement from the past week

- Plan and lead a game or activity

- Prepare and serve refreshments

This approach is not to be overwhelming for parent or child; rather, it is an opportunity to give a child special attention and for each to be granted "equal privilege." It involves all the senses as we behold one another. Those with young children may need to adjust their expectation for attentive listeners to participate in a "family home moment" lesson rather than a family home evening lesson. When we had young children, we gave each the opportunity to "read" the scriptures by repeating a few lines after us. Very soon, one child learned some of the oft-repeated phrases and words and determined to read the scriptures herself. She would track her finger left to right across the page and say, "And it came to pass" over and over again. She felt so big and important!

Families do not need to include every item listed above. Pick from the list what works best for you and your current situation. Be wise and sensitive to the needs and attention span of your children and your ability to nurture them. No matter the situation, if the expectations are too high, if the experiences together are too often disagreeable, if there is too much harshness and not enough kindness, ask yourself, "Would you want to be your child right now?" Whether at family home evenings, at the dinner table, in interviews, or during informal conversations, our goal should be to wrap our child in the blanket of caring, confidence, safety, and joy. Parents who follow this pattern of parenting will rear their children with their love and the love of their Heavenly Father.

Parenting principles from Christ and the Nephites: Take the time and effort to "behold" the one. Spend time informally and formally to connect with each child and value his or her worth as Christ did. Give each child opportunities to participate and listen to others in the family that all may learn and be edified by each other.

NOTES

1. M. Russell Ballard, "Great Shall Be the Peace of Thy Children," *Ensign,* April 1994, 59.

2.   Robert D. Hales, "Our Duty to God: The Mission of Parents and Leaders to the Rising Generation," *Ensign,* May 2010, 95.

3.   David A. Bednar, "Watching with All Perseverance," *Ensign,* May 2010, 41.

4.   Larry R. Lawrence, "Courageous Parenting," *Ensign,* November 2010, 100.

5.   Robert D. Hales, "Our Duty to God: The Mission of Parents and Leaders to the Rising Generation," *Ensign,* May 2010, 97.

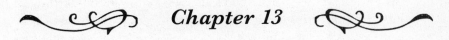

Chapter 13

JACOB AND HIS TWELVE SONS: THE POWER OF FORGIVENESS

After the prophet Jacob spoke to the Nephite congregation, he wrote, "We labor diligently to engraven these words on plates, hoping that . . . our children will receive them with thankful hearts, and look upon them that they may learn with joy and not with sorrow, neither with contempt, concerning their first parents" (Jacob 4:3). Jacob's words touch my heart. I am certain good parents feel as Jacob did. We want our children to realize we are human but are doing our best. We wish our children to look past our mistakes and forgive our weaknesses in parenting.

Another Book of Mormon prophet ended his writings similarly: "Condemn me not because of mine imperfection, neither my father, because of his imperfection . . . but rather give thanks unto God that he hath made manifest unto you our imperfections, *that ye may learn to be more wise than we have been*" (Mormon 9:31; emphasis added). The scriptures contain resplendent examples of parents who had great hardships in life but desired to do their best at parenting. We read of some mistakes and how they repented. These parents are great people who show us how to forgive when they are offended and how to not be provoked to anger.

Another Jacob, a patriarch in the Old Testament, was renamed "Israel." He fathered twelve sons who became the progenitors of the twelve tribes of Israel. Their family story is poignant and one of enmity and reconciliation. Joseph was Jacob's favored son, who learned through dreams that he was chosen of God to lead his family. When he told his older brothers he would rule over them, "they hated him yet the more for his dreams, and for his words" (Genesis 37:8). Joseph was wronged by these brothers who "could not speak peaceable unto him" (Genesis 37:4), yet he bore their wrath in meekness.

The abusive brothers' hatred and jealousy grew toward this birthright son until they staged his death and sold him to a traveling band of Ishmaelites. He was launched into a foreign, hostile land and years of severe trials. Joseph, however, endured his hardships with equanimity and faith. Eventually, he became the means by which Egypt and the surrounding areas (including his own family) were saved from a seven-year famine. When he was reunited with his brothers after twenty-two years, Joseph freely forgave them for the great wrong committed against him and gathered the entire family to enjoy prosperity in Egypt.

Jacob, their father, continued to set the standard of reconciliation between his children. They lived peaceably together in Egypt, but when Jacob died, the older brothers were afraid Joseph would revisit the evil they had done to him. They sent a messenger to Joseph to deliver the final words their father had commanded of his children: "So shall ye say unto Joseph, Forgive, I pray thee now, the trespass of thy brethren, and their sin; for they did unto thee evil" (Genesis 50:17). The brothers supplicated Joseph, "And now, we pray thee, forgive the trespass of the servants of the God of thy father" (Genesis 50:17).

Joseph, who had demonstrated unwavering charity toward his once-contemptuous brothers, wept before them once again. This signaled their family's final spiritual reconciliation, a tribute to their patriarch father's dying wishes. Joseph's brothers bowed before their younger brother and said, "Behold, we be thy servants" (Genesis 50:18). Joseph's revelatory words foreshadowed the mission of the Savior: "Fear not: for am I [not] in the place of God? But as for you, ye thought evil against me; but God meant it unto good, to bring to pass, as it is this day, to save much people alive. Now therefore fear ye not: I will nourish you, and your little ones" (Genesis 50:19–21). Joseph was a type of Christ, saving a fallen nation from physical death but, more important, offering spiritual healing to repentant brothers who had committed extreme hostility against him.

Moroni and Pahoran, two steadfast friends in the Book of Mormon, are also examples of repentance and forgiveness. Both were leaders in a great ongoing war and were separated by distance and means of reliable communication. Moroni was chief captain of the army at the battlefield; Pahoran was the chief judge and governor in the city of Zarahemla. At the apex of a war between the Nephites and Lamanites, the Nephites experienced a faction among themselves. A group calling themselves "king-men" rose up in rebellion and usurped the government. This weakened the Nephite's ability to fight without when there was strife within. Pahoran was taken out of power, and no support or supplies were sent to aid the troops. Moroni was not made aware of the insurrection, and he and his troops suffered tremendously.

Moroni wrote an epistle and condemned what he felt was a reprehensible lack of aid. Unfortunately, he was unaware of the facts of the matter and directed his wrath toward Pahoran. In anger, Moroni blamed his compatriot with "exceedingly great neglect": "Can you think to sit upon your thrones in a state of thoughtless stupor while your enemies are spreading the work of death around you?" (Alma 60:6–7). He accused Pahoran of many harsh deeds such as being a traitor to his country, slothfulness, pride and ambition, trampling the commandments underfoot, and great wickedness that would incur the judgments of God.

These are strident words indeed! How easily Pahoran could have been offended! He was unjustly accused by a "beloved brother" and equally patriotic countryman. In Pahoran's response epistle, we find a benevolent, generous example of how to forgive. He explained the realities of his harrowing situation and said, "And now, in your epistle you have censured me, but *it mattereth not*; I am not angry, but do rejoice in the greatness of your heart" (Alma 61:9; emphasis added). Pahoran knew Moroni was motivated by love of family and country and had simply misdirected his zeal. He did not take his attack personally; instead, he saw the intent of his heart and freely forgave him.

It mattereth not. These words by Pahoran should be the guiding principle in parenting when unintended offense is given. Pahoran did not match fire with fire but dissipated the emotion with understanding. He knew "a soft answer turneth away wrath: but grievous words stir up anger" (Proverbs 15:1). More familial relationships today need the healing words, "It just doesn't matter."

Helaman fought with his young warriors during the same period as Moroni, suffering from lack of aid as well. He was ignorant of the struggles the government had with the king-men and why he and his men were left "to perish for the want of food" (Alma 58:7). Yet Helaman's reaction was not anger. He affirmed, "We do not desire to murmur" (Alma 58:35). He wondered what the possibilities were for the neglect but gave his leaders the benefit of the doubt. Along with Pahoran, he let go of the injustice, saying, "It mattereth not" (Alma 58:37). The injustice was inconsequential because Helaman recognized that despite not knowing everything, he knew this: "We trust God will deliver us, notwithstanding the weakness of our armies, yea, and deliver us out of the hands of our enemies" (Alma 58:37). Helaman's meek and faithful attitude can be ours if we just remember to let go of things that do not matter and trust in God.

When our relationship with our children is at stake, we cannot let anger be the fuel to burn between us. Elder Juan A. Uceda shared this honest parenting experience in general conference:

> One morning a family gathered to study the scriptures as usual. As they gathered, the father felt a negative spirit: some members of the family did not look very excited to participate. They had family prayer, and as they started to read the scriptures, the father noticed that one of the children did not have her personal set of scriptures with her. He invited her to go to her room and bring her scriptures. She reluctantly did so, and after a period of time that seemed like an eternity, she returned, sat down, and said, "Do we really have to do this now?
>
> The father thought to himself that the enemy of all righteousness wanted to create problems so that they would not study the scriptures. The father, trying to stay calm, said, "Yes, we have to do this now because this is what the Lord wants us to do.
>
> She responded, "I don't really want to do this now!"
>
> The father then lost his patience, raised his voice, and said, "This is my home, and we will always read the scriptures in my home!"
>
> The tone and volume of his words hurt his daughter, and with her scriptures in hand, she left the family circle, ran to her bedroom, and slammed the door. Thus ended the family scripture study—no harmony and little love being felt at home.
>
> The father knew that he had done wrong, so he went to his own bedroom and knelt down to pray. He pleaded with the Lord for help, knowing that he had offended one of His children, a daughter whom he truly loved. He implored the Lord to restore the spirit of love and harmony at home and enable them to be able to continue studying the scriptures as a family. As he was praying, an idea came to his mind: "Go and say, 'I'm sorry.'" He continued to pray earnestly, asking for the Spirit of the Lord to come back into his home. Once again the idea came: "Go back and say, 'I'm sorry.'"

He really wanted to be a good father and do the right thing, so he stood up and went to his daughter's bedroom. He gently knocked on the door several times, and there was no answer. So he slowly opened the door and found his girl sobbing and crying on her bed. He kneeled next to her and said with a soft and tender voice, "I'm sorry. I apologize for what I did." He repeated, "I'm sorry, I love you, and I don't want to hurt you." And then from the mouth of a child came the lesson that the Lord wanted to teach him.

She stopped crying, and after a brief silence, she took her scriptures into her hands and started to look up some verses. The father watched as those pure and delicate hands turned the pages of the scriptures, page after page. She came to the verses she sought and started to read very slowly with a soft voice: "For the natural man is an enemy to God, and has been from the fall of Adam, and will be, forever and ever, unless he yields to the enticings of the Holy Spirit, and putteth off the natural man and becometh a saint through the atonement of Christ the Lord, and becometh as a child, submissive, meek, humble, patient, full of love, willing to submit to all things which the Lord seeth fit to inflict upon him, even as a child doth submit to his father" [Mosiah 3:19].

While he was still kneeling next to her bed, humility overcame him as he thought to himself, "That scripture was written for me. She has taught me a great lesson."

Then she turned her eyes to him and said, "I am sorry. I am sorry, Daddy."

At that very moment the father realized she did not read that verse to apply that scripture to him, but she read it applying it to herself. He opened his arms and embraced her. Love and harmony had been restored in this sweet moment of reconciliation born of the word of God and the Holy Ghost. That scripture, which his daughter remembered from her own personal scripture study, had touched his heart with the fire of the Holy Ghost.[1]

An angry child is a discouraged child. "Fathers, provoke not your children to anger, lest they be discouraged" (Colossians 3:21). We need to look past the strong emotion and see what they are really saying. What needs are we not meeting? How can we be more understanding or exercise compromise? Are they lacking in our attention or love? "Therefore, strengthen your brethren in all your conversation, in all your prayers, in all your exhortations, and in all your doings" (D&C 108:7). We are commanded to *strengthen* each other, not tear family members down with hurtful, harsh words and unchecked emotions. "And now my brethren,

I judge these things of you because of your peaceable walk with the children of men" (Moroni 7:4).

My mother often used humor to defuse the tension between family members when someone became angry at another. I remember her saying during a sibling quarrel, "Did you hear that?" and we stopped for a moment to listen. She continued with a smile, "It was the door slamming shut as the Holy Ghost just left our house." Or she would begin singing the words to the hymn, "Let us oft speak kind words to each other."[2] President Gordon B. Hinckley gave this charge:

> This brings me to another area where there is so great a need for that mercy which speaks of forbearance, kindness, clemency, compassion. I speak of the homes of the people.
>
> Every child, with few possible exceptions, is the product of a home, be it good, bad, or indifferent. As children grow through the years, their lives, in large measure, become an extension and a reflection of family teaching. If there is harshness, abuse, uncontrolled anger, disloyalty, the fruits will be certain and discernible, and in all likelihood they will be repeated in the generation that follows. If, on the other hand, there is forbearance, forgiveness, respect, consideration, kindness, mercy, and compassion, the fruits again will be discernible, and they will be eternally rewarding. They will be positive and sweet and wonderful. And as mercy is given and taught by parents, it will be repeated in the lives and actions of the next generation.
>
> I speak to fathers and mothers everywhere with a plea to put harshness behind us, to bridle our anger, to lower our voices, and to deal with mercy and love and respect one toward another in our homes. . . .
>
> Let us be more merciful. Let us get the arrogance out of our lives, the conceit, the egotism. Let us be more compassionate, gentler, filled with forbearance and patience and a greater measure of respect one for another. In so doing, our very example will cause others to be more merciful, and we shall have greater claim upon the mercy of God who in His love will be generous toward us.[3]

Having patience and a milder temperament are parenting attributes I am earnestly trying to turn from personal weaknesses to strengths. I have worked over the years to not become as reactive to my children's mistakes and to control my temper. One of my daughters tends to be impetuous by nature. In the past, I repeated in frustration at her mishaps, "Slow down! Look where you are going!" or "Pay attention to what you are doing!" Unfortunately, I fell into a pattern of berating her for unintended mistakes, which damaged her confidence. I became frustrated, and so did she.

A few years ago, my husband and I took our eldest daughter on a trip to Italy. One of the places we visited was Deruta, a quaint town famous for its potters and artisans. We toured a centuries-old pottery factory, where ceramics and handmade tableware start as raw clay and are finished as exquisite pieces of art in their storefront. We bought a beautiful serving tray, and I hand-carried it home as a treasured souvenir.

A year or so later, Rachel, our impulsive twelve-year-old daughter, was cooking in the kitchen and reached up to retrieve a baking dish out of a high cupboard. In her haste, she inadvertently pulled out the Italian platter and it fell onto the floor and shattered into hundreds of pieces. I heard the crash and immediately saw what had happened. I was devastated . . . and angry. Our only souvenir was gone. My first reaction was to yell, "Haven't I told you a million times to be more careful?" but I didn't. Thankfully, I held my peace and walked out of the room to cool down. Rachel stayed in the kitchen to sweep up all the shards. I was upset for a while but soon got over the loss. However, I was still a bit irritated that she never apologized.

About two months later, it was my birthday, and I received two presents from Rachel. I opened the first, and to my astonishment, she gave me the Italian plate . . . with all the pieces glued back together. *Wow.* I don't know how long it had taken her but it must have been incredibly difficult to piece it all back by herself. I sat there in utter amazement and disbelief. My eyes filled with tears. I was so ashamed by my quick condemnation of her. Inside the handmade birthday card, she had written,

> Dear Mom,
>   I am so sorry. I really didn't see it in the cupboard. Thanks for not getting mad at me. I tried to re-piece it (as you can tell), but it is still hideous. You can throw it away or whatever you want.
>
>   Love, Rachel

The second birthday gift was another serving dish she had bought with her own babysitting money. I was *so thankful* at that moment that I had not rushed to vent my anger and offend this tender girl. When I had regained my composure, I thanked her and told her that the glued-together plate was more precious to me than the perfect one we had brought home from Italy. It represented the cracks and faults we share as a family and that love is the glue that binds us together. No family is perfect, just like the plate, but we are better and more beautiful when we forgive. I treasure that plate! Now, whenever I feel an irritation welling toward a child, I remember the Italian plate and my sweet, penitent daughter.

Robert D. Hales spoke of the imperfections of families and the need to forgive through the Atonement of Jesus Christ. We conclude with his counsel:

> I want to remind all of us today that no family has reached perfection. All families are subject to the conditions of mortality. All of us are given the gift of agency—to choose for ourselves and to learn from the consequences of our choices.
>
> Any of us may experience a spouse, a child, a parent, or a member of our extended family suffering in one way or another—mentally, physically, emotionally, or spiritually—and we may experience these tribulations ourselves at times. In short, mortality is not easy.
>
> Each family has its own special circumstances. But the gospel of Jesus Christ addresses every challenge—which is why we must teach it to our children.[4]

Parenting principles from Jacob and his twelve sons: No family is perfect. Each member is in need of patience as we make mistakes and try to become better. Peace, forbearance, and kindness should govern our speech and actions. Provoking a child to anger engenders discouragement and damage to the parent-child relationship. Anger has no place in a home where we desire the companionship of the Holy Ghost.

NOTES

1. Juan A. Uceda, "He Teaches Us to Put Off the Natural Man," *Ensign,* November 2010, 53.

2. "Let Us Oft Speak Kind Words," *Hymns,* no. 232.

3. Gordon B. Hinckley, "Blessed Are the Merciful," *Ensign,* May 1990, 70.

4. Robert D. Hales, "A Message of Hope to Families," *Ensign,* May 2004, 88.

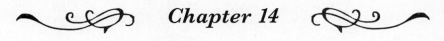

Chapter 14

JOSEPH AND MARY: THE POWER OF TEMPLES

What would parents think if you were to offer them a blueprint for raising their child? What price would they pay? How far would they travel to obtain it? Nephi, a prophet in the Book of Mormon, showed us where to find it. There is no better formula for raising a child than comparing it with the "blueprint" he received to build a ship. Nephi and his family crossed the waters to the promised land in a ship whose workmanship was unprecedented. It was not after "the manner which was learned by men, neither did I build the ship after the manner of men; but I did build it after the manner which the Lord had shown unto me" (1 Nephi 18:2). There is a type in this story for parents who recognize the singular nature of raising a child.

Each child that comes to us is unique; there are no two children alike. Neither is there a way we can duplicate how we raise one child to another. Each requires a fresh approach with individual treatment and consideration, just like building an original ship. There were no standardized blueprints Nephi brought with him from Jerusalem that he used for this special vessel. Indeed, this one was to take them across the sea into uncharted territory.

Uncharted territory. Does this sound a bit like raising a child? And once you have "mapped out" the directions to raise a young child, they grow into an alien adolescent or another child joins the family with new

113

coordinates! Perhaps Nephi felt quite overwhelmed at his task. He had never constructed a ship before; in fact, his brothers mocked him for even trying. What does Nephi write in the next verse to show us how he accomplished it? "And I, Nephi, did go into the mount oft, and I did pray oft unto the Lord; wherefore the Lord showed unto me great things" (1 Nephi 18:3). I imagine he went "oft" because the Lord's blueprints were not revealed all at once. As is common to the Lord's economy, Nephi received revelation "line upon line, precept upon precept" (2 Nephi 28:30) as he was ready and able to understand and apply each concept as it was given.

The temples are our "mounts" today where we can go, like Nephi, to learn how to raise each child entrusted to our care. He received the "blueprint" needed for ship-building just as we can learn "great things" about raising our children. There is inspiration in the house of the Lord. There is serenity. We are more able to hear His voice saying, "Be still and know that I am God" (Psalms 46: 10).

The temple endows us with the ability to teach our children about the Savior Jesus Christ, our relationship to him and to each other. Through our temple service, our children can find great peace and power in His word. "And all thy children shall be taught of the Lord; and great shall be the peace of thy children" (Isaiah 54:13). Another word about peace that Christ taught his disciples: "Peace I leave with you, my peace I give unto you. Not as the world giveth give I unto you. Let not your hearts be troubled, neither let it be afraid" (John 14:27). Elder Jeffrey R. Holland elaborated about this scripture in John:

> I submit to you, that may be one of the Savior's commandments that is, even in the hearts of otherwise faithful Latter-day Saints, almost universally disobeyed; and yet I wonder whether our resistance to this invitation could be any more grievous to the Lord's merciful heart. I can tell you this as a parent: as concerned as I would be if somewhere in their lives one of my children were seriously troubled or unhappy or disobedient, nevertheless I would be infinitely more devastated if I felt that at such a time that child could not trust me to help or thought his or her interest was unimportant to me or unsafe in my care. In that same spirit, I am convinced that none of us can appreciate how deeply it wounds the loving heart of the Savior of the world when he finds that his people do not feel confident in his care or secure in his hands or trust in his commandments.[1]

We are commanded to have peace, not fear, in this world. Parenthood may have troubling times, but we can find true peace through the Comforter, covenants in the temple, and the word of God.

Joseph and Mary, parents of the Holy Child, were exemplary in temple worship and following the Spirit as they raised Jesus, their firstborn son. When Christ was eight days old, they took him to the temple in Jerusalem to present him to God. Under the law of Moses, they offered sacrifice of two turtledoves and obeyed the law of circumcision. On that sacred ground, they were blessed with a remarkable spiritual manifestation.

Anna and Simeon were the two elderly visionaries who spoke to Joseph and Mary while at the temple. Anna, the widow of eighty-four years, "departed not from the temple, but served God with fastings and prayers night and day" (Luke 2:37). Simeon was equally "just and devout, waiting for the consolation of Israel: and the Holy Ghost was upon him" (Luke 2:25). When Mary and Joseph brought their child to them, the Spirit rested upon Simeon and Anna, and they prophesied to these new parents about the divinity of their Son, his Messiahship, his death, and the salvation of Israel through him. Simeon blessed them and "Joseph and his mother marvelled at those things which were spoken of him" (Luke 2:33). Truly, they were shown "great things"! How blessed they were to have been in the temple that day, fulfilling their duty as parents.

Twelve years later, and after many visits to the temple, Joseph and Mary once again traveled to Jerusalem for the Feast of the Passover. On their return home, Jesus's parents discovered he was not with the party. How interesting that Luke did not write that Jesus was accidentally left behind, lost in a crowded city as we often surmise. Instead he wrote, "The child Jesus tarried behind in Jerusalem; and Joseph and his mother knew not of it" (Luke 2:43). "To tarry" means to intentionally stay behind—to linger, expecting something. The frantic parents returned and searched the city. Jesus was found where he had chosen to tarry: in the temple. The boy Jesus had been taught by his parents that one can draw near to our Father in Heaven in His house. He was certain "the Lord is in his holy temple" (Psalm 11:4).

Indeed, Jesus had never been "lost." He knew where he needed to be. Likewise, our children will not be spiritually lost if their goal is to be found in the temple. Parents can prioritize doing baptisms by proxy with their adolescent children as often as possible. We can visit the temple grounds with young children, testifying of the beauty found therein.

Children can choose a picture of a temple to hang in their bedroom. With lessons of temple worship from Joseph and Mary, "Jesus increased in wisdom and stature, and in favour with God and man" (Luke 2:52). Inspiration found in the temple helps us raise our children in all these necessary areas of growth and development: intellectually, physically, spiritually, and socially.

Isaiah described temples using a symbol of supreme significance. "And it shall come to pass in the last days, that the mountain of the Lord's house shall be established in the top of the mountains, and shall be exalted above the hills; and all nations shall flow unto it" (Isaiah 2:2). Why is a temple called a "mountain" and is placed *on* a mountain? Employing a double metaphor strengthens the message to us.

When we hike up a mountain, it is symbolic of temple worship. The ascension physically brings us closer to the heavens, where God is. As waters flow down the mountain, we are flowing up. We reach the summit by compassing the lower regions, much like advancing from lower to higher degrees of glory. Moses followed this progressive pattern in Exodus chapter 24 as he climbed the levels of Mount Sinai. We become removed from the world, breathing cleaner air and feeling cleansed from the underlying pollutions. The further we are from Babylon below, the more we gain perspective. Worldly objects shrink into nothingness. Accordingly, we see more from above, and things that loomed large down below do not appear so ominous.

Those on the hike are unified in their purpose; we are not bankers, electricians, musicians, or veterinarians anymore—we are all on a common trail, just hikers with a friendly wave and smile to all we pass. Additionally, the hike itself takes effort, and hikers make deliberate plans beforehand and ready themselves for the journey. Gaining a temple recommend takes effort, and attending the temple requires preparation. Elder David E. Sorensen defined the "work" in temple work: "While the temple is certainly a place of refuge, a retreat to learn and understand ourselves, there may be even more benefit in going to the temple to actually do exacting, weighty, rigorous, demanding work."[2]

When we reach the mountaintop, hikers will usually stop to relish the view, to rest and eat a snack before descending. We find joy, rest, and refreshment in the ordinances and covenants performed in the temple. Quoting Elder Sorensen again: "The temple is a place of revelation, of inspiration, meditation, and peace—a place to restore ourselves, to clear our minds, to find answers to our prayers, and to enjoy the satisfaction of worship and service."[3] Most transcendent of all, the "mountain" (temple) is established on a "mountain" because temples and the covenants therein are founded on the Rock, our Redeemer, Jesus Christ.

Our prophet today is advancing the work of establishing temples throughout the world so all members may have easier access to a house of the Lord. Concerning the responsibility of parents to attend the temple, Thomas S. Monson said, "I plead with you to teach your children of the temple's importance. The world can be a challenging and difficult place in which to live. We are often surrounded by that which would drag us down. As you and I go to the holy houses of God, as we remember the covenants we make within, we will be more able to bear every trial and to overcome each temptation. In this sacred sanctuary we will find peace; we will be renewed and fortified."[4]

Temples are houses of the Lord. Holy help is available there. He declared, "Fear thou not; for I am with thee: be not dismayed; for I am thy God: I will strengthen thee; yea, I will help thee; yea, I will uphold thee with the right hand of my righteousness" (Isaiah 41:10). The veil is thin as work is being done simultaneously on both sides.

Turning to the scriptures, we find how close heaven is and how solicitous angels are of our needs. One example comes from Elisha in the Old Testament. When the king of Syria attacked the Israelites, they were rebuffed several times. The king learned there was a prophet among the Israelites, so he sent a large army to surround Dotham and destroy the city where Elisha was living. Early the next morning, Elisha's servant saw the formidable forces preparing for battle and was plagued by despair. Elisha prayed for the Lord to open the young man's eyes, and this is what he saw: "Behold, the mountain was full of horses and chariots and fire round about Elisha" (2 Kings 6:17). When we feel alone and helpless, the temple is holy ground where we can ponder Elisha's promise: "Fear not: for they that be with us are more than they that be with them" (2 Kings 6:16). A legion of heavenly help is near.

I once experienced the temple's thin veil and how the other side is anxious to help. While our son was preparing to become a full-time missionary, he encountered progress and setbacks as he prepared to receive a recommend and be issued a call. When the day finally came that we entered those holy doors together and he received his endowment, my heart was full. No words could describe the tremendous gratitude to the

Lord for redeeming my son and getting him to that point. We were fortunate to have my in-laws with us for this ordinance, and my father-in-law wrote me later of an impression he received in the temple. He said, "As we were leaving the celestial room, I offered a prayer of thanks for all that had been done to this point. I had one of those moments that occasionally occurs in the temple—a prompt answer of *'Yes, we have been working on this for some time.'* He will not be alone."

A couple I greatly admire lost their young child to a terrible accident. I remember the day it happened and running over to her house. She and her husband stood outside their house—in the very spot where their son had just been taken—and I witnessed them comforting those who had arrived and sharing their testimony of the gospel. Her husband offered guests to come inside to "feel the Spirit in our home right now." In their grief, they shared the outpouring of the Spirit. This friend shared her feelings with me:

> *The day Cooper died was too overwhelming to take in. We were flooded by people but also flooded by the Holy Ghost. These two sources of strength held us up during those day's events. When night fell, my husband and I couldn't sleep. We got out of bed and went outside on the front porch before the sun rose and just talked, shared, held each other, and cried. From our porch, we could see the temple in the valley below. Everything was still quite dark and the temple was literally the brightest thing we could see. We looked at each other and said, "We need to go. We need to go right now."*
>
> *Before the sun even came up, we went to the sealing room and were reminded how our family was born under the covenant, sealed together for eternity and that we could claim Cooper forever if we stayed worthy. It was the only place we could go to draw nearer to heaven and understand Heavenly Father's plan for us—that He is completely in charge. We recognized those feelings of peace instantaneously because we had felt the Spirit so many times before in our lives. We knew the Holy Ghost could guide us through whatever lay ahead.*
>
> *The Spirit sustained us during those initial days. I marvel how I didn't despair at the time of losing Cooper. Those feelings came later when the reality of the loss became so profound. When pain washes over me in moments of despair, I have to work to gain my strength back and remind myself of the hope we have through Christ's Atonement—that we can all live again as families.*
>
> *Losing Cooper has had such a profound effect on our family. Our priorities have been altered. My husband and I attend the temple much more frequently to replenish ourselves with the sacred serenity that carries*

us from day to day. We have even taken detours on vacations just to attend the temple. My husband has not missed a week of attending the temple since losing our little boy. He knows his purpose in mortality is to prepare to be with Cooper again and the temple helps us to do that. He knows his eternal salvation is dependent upon his renewal of covenants and he has followed through no matter how busy or demanding his weekly schedule can be. The temple has saved us.

Not only did Nephi climb to his holy mount to receive instruction, he "cried unto the Lord" (1 Nephi 17:7). The psalmist said, "In my distress I called upon the Lord, and cried unto my God: he heard my voice out of his temple and my cry came before him, even into his ears" (Psalms 18:6; see also 2 Samuel 22:7). In the temple our deepest longings are expressed and heard. We return home strengthened. In the dedicatory prayer offered by Joseph Smith at the Kirtland Temple, he pled, "And we ask thee, Holy Father, that thy servants may go forth with thy power, and that thy name may be upon them, and thy glory be round about them, and thine angels have charge over them" (D&C 109:22). Another favorite scripture of mine where the Lord is speaking brings comfort to us as well: "I will go before your face, I will be on your right hand and on your left, and my Spirit shall be in your hearts, and mine angels round about you, to bear you up" (D&C 84:88).

My sister "cried unto the Lord" many times when her son was serving a mission. She pondered many times the promise of protecting angels in Doctrine and Covenants. Her temple attendance and earnest prayers summoned tremendous blessings for their family. She recounts such a miracle:

All during Michael's mission, I was worried because he was serving in a very dangerous area in Peru. I kept thinking, "I wish I could pierce the veil and see how the Lord protects his missionaries. I wonder how unseen angels surround and protect His servants and how the heavens operate in that respect." I mused over this question many times.

My husband and I went to pick him up when the two years had ended. We arrived two days before his release, and because his companion had already left, we were assigned to be his companions. Michael was assigned to live in the most dangerous part of the mission; a great portion of the locals carried guns. Shootings and murders were a part of daily life. Taxi drivers wouldn't drive to his apartment out of fear. So we walked into his neighborhood with him during the day, but we couldn't carry anything.

The last night of his mission, he had a baptism. It was scheduled in the evening after church, so we did not arrive at his apartment to move him out until 9:30 p.m. By 10:00 p.m. we were ready to leave. We were left to carry all his belongings into the street and walk for many blocks before we could even find a taxi to pick us up. We looked down below on the street and saw gangs clustering outside. It was a frightening experience at that time of night.

Then, like angels, we saw ward members beginning to assemble at the bottom of the stairs. When they all arrived, there were probably 15–20 people. Two men took Michael's luggage, a mother handed my husband her baby, and a little girl, about six-years-old, approached and took my hand. They offered themselves as a shield and protection. When we came out onto the street, the ward members surrounded us, and we walked down the street completely enveloped within this circle of safety. As we walked the dark streets past the menacing gang members eyeing us at every corner, I had this thought: "You got your wish. You now see how angels protect the missionaries." It was electrifying. My husband and I were both crying. We felt the Spirit so strongly. We were walking on sacred ground.

The words of Elder Dennis B. Neuenschwander sum up this chapter. He counseled:

Amidst the bustle of the secular world, with its certain uncertainty, there must be places that offer spiritual refuge, renewal, hope, and peace. There are indeed such places. They are both holy and sacred. They are places where we meet the divine and find the Spirit of the Lord. . . . In holy places and in sacred space we find spiritual refuge, renewal, hope, and peace. Are these not worth every necessary personal sacrifice? My brethren and sisters, may each of us revere and respect the holy and sacred in our lives. May we teach our children likewise. Let us all stand in holy and sacred places of spiritual peace.[5]

As we attend the temples often, the Lord will give us peace *and*— piece by piece—the tools, materials, and blueprint for raising each child. What price will we pay to get to the temple? How far are we willing to travel to get there? We can gain inspiration about how to build up our children, to see them grow and take shape, until each is ready to set sail on uncharted waters.

Parenting principles from Joseph and Mary: Each child is unique. We must attend to each according to their individual needs. Since we cannot parent each child exactly the same, we must seek for the Lord's blueprints through constant prayer, study, fasting, and temple attendance.

Temples are the house of the Lord where he will reveal peace to our hearts and inspiration to our minds about our stewardship as parents. Our example of temple service will teach our children they will never be lost if they are found in the temple.

NOTES

1.   Jeffrey R. Holland, "Come unto Me," *Ensign,* April 1998, 19.

2.   David E. Sorensen, "The Doctrine of Temple Work," *Ensign,* October 2003, 58.

3.   Sorensen, "The Doctrine of Temple Work," 60.

4.   Thomas S. Monson, "The Holy Temple—A Beacon to the World," *Ensign,* May 2011, 93.

5.   Dennis B. Neuenschwander, "Holy Place, Sacred Space," *Ensign,* May 2003, 71–72.

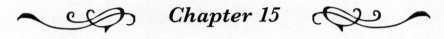

Chapter 15

JOSHUA AND THE TWELVE STONES: THE POWER OF MEMORIALS

While I was growing up, my dad was a professor of mechanical engineering at Oregon State University. Every day, I saw him take his leather briefcase to work and bring it home again. Back in those days, teachers graded actual papers with actual red pencils, not electronically like we do most of our work today. Sometimes I'd ask if he'd let me mark the score at the top of the page (I felt so important!), and he'd let me. His quiet example of everyday small, simple acts inspired me to be a teacher. I even sat in on one of his lectures. I had no idea what they were talking about (what is the Navier-Stokes equation anyway?) but he framed many memories for me. Now I carry my own briefcase when I teach. He is retired from teaching, and I asked him for that old leather briefcase, which I now own. What does that briefcase represent to me? Sacrifice. Hard work. Love. Diligence. Commitment. Joshua from the Old Testament is an example of how tangible objects can carry powerful meaning.

Joshua became the next prophet, father figure, and patriarch to the children of Israel after Moses's death. He was granted the blessing denied Moses of crossing the River Jordan into the promised land. The priests bore the ark of the covenant that held the commandments written on tablets. When they approached the River Jordan, they had to navigate it while safely carrying the ark above water. All who were present witnessed a miracle similar to the crossing of the Red Sea. With faith, the priests stepped out into the water and it rose on both sides, reminiscent of the Red Sea parting. It is a wonder they did not waiver as they took that leap of faith out into deep water. The scripture affirms the priests "stood firm on dry ground in the midst of Jordan" (Joshua 3:17) carrying the sacred ark. In turn, all the Israelites were able to cross on dry ground to the other side.

Joshua knew the power of visuals. After crossing the River Jordan, he called twelve men, one representing each tribe, to take a stone where the priests' feet stood firm. Joshua instructed them to carry the stones across the river and lay them on the other side. "That this may be a sign among you, that when your children ask their fathers in time to come, saying, What mean ye by these stones? Then ye shall answer them, That the waters of Jordan were cut off before the Ark of the Covenant of the Lord; when it passed over Jordan, the waters of Jordan were cut off: and these stones shall be for a memorial unto the children of Israel for ever" (Joshua 4:6–7).

These twelve ordinary stones took on a symbolic significance of the power of God. Memories of miracles and testimonies may fade unless there are reminders. These stones marked the spot and "they are there unto this day" (Joshua 4:9). I can envision Israelite families taking their children back to the spot and saying, "Here it was where we saw the waters part and the priests carry the ark on dry ground." The twelve stones each represented a tribe, or family, that was present. The children might have touched the stone and been touched again in their hearts. They could have pictured how one of those stones belonged to "them" and how they were connected to this miracle.

Alma the Younger's righteousness was rooted in this proclamation: "Yea, I have *always* remembered" (Alma 29:12; emphasis added; see also Alma 36:29). How can we unite the feelings our children experience with something tangible they remember later? We find many examples embedded in scripture stories. The ark was not the only visual source of strength for the children of Israel. Moses's staff that parted the Red Sea and that he held up (with the aid of Aaron and Hur) was a reminder of God's power as they prevailed against Amalek's army (see Exodus 17: 8–12). Moses raised a pole affixed with a brass serpent that the children of Israel might see and believe on a symbol of Christ's atoning healing (Numbers 21:6–9; see also Alma 33:19–21).

The children of the newly converted Lamanites, who called themselves the Anti-Nephi-Lehies, were witnesses to their parents' dramatic demonstration of faith and change of heart. They gathered together in a ceremonial covenant and dug a large pit in which to place all their weapons of war. They resolved never to shed blood again. They watched their fathers solemnly lay down these symbols of their former life and bury them as a witness to their absolute conversion. That must have become a consecrated spot where those children remembered their parents promising, "We will bury them deep in the earth, that they may be kept bright, as a testimony that we have never used them, at the last day; and if our brethren destroy us, behold, we shall go to our God and shall be saved" (Alma 24:16).

A miraculous event parallel to the Red Sea parting was the Jaredites crossing the ocean in barges. Particularly the people of Jared knew the mighty hand of God. He guided their vessels through perilous waters and safely landed them on the shores of the promised land. God did not literally part the waters, as his did for the Israelites, but He created a path through the waters, carved by providential winds. "The Lord God caused that there should be a furious wind blow upon the face of the waters, towards the promised land. . . the wind did never cease to blow towards the promised land while they were upon the waters" (Ether 6:5, 8). The journey lasted nearly a year.

It is no surprise the family of Jared grew prosperous in their new land as they held this experience fresh in memory. It would seem impossible to forget such a marvelous, harrowing event. I can imagine these family members telling and retelling their children and grandchildren about traversing the waters, the gratitude they felt for their preserved lives, and for the land preserved for their inheritance. Remembering their divine deliverance caused the brother of Jared's son Orihah to remain righteous. He was the only son to accept the position as king, the first king of their primitive American settlement. Ether 6:30, the last verse in this chapter, ends with: "And it came to pass that Orihah did walk humbly before the Lord, and *did remember* how great things the Lord had done for his fathers and also *taught his people how great things the Lord had done for their fathers*" (emphasis added). These stories were recorded in the scriptures so after the first generation died, the story of the miracle did not die with them. They created something concrete to jog their memory . . . and their faithfulness.

A few generations later, another descendant of Jared was named Shule. He lived in troubled and wicked times. However, he is one of the few righteous in that generation and reigned as king of the Jaredites. There are scant details in the book of Ether of why he was righteous while others were not—but namely this: "And there were no more wars in the days of Shule; and he remembered the great things that the Lord had done for his fathers in bringing them across the great deep into the promised land; wherefore he did execute judgment in righteousness all his days" (Ether 7:27). The word *wherefore* speaks loudly to me. It is the linking word between *cause* (remembering) and *effect* (righteousness). Shule remembered the miraculous deliverance of his fathers; wherefore (in other words, because of that vivid, daily memory), he remained righteous. The scripture tied his goodness directly to one act: his conscious choice of remembering his fathers. As king, with immense power and opportunity to abuse his position, he could have easily fallen into temptation and wickedness. On the contrary, that one scripture addressed a core reason why he remained faithful. Passing down lessons of gratitude for our forefathers, our personal blessings, and the daily tender mercies we experience are necessary for our children to remain faithful.

We create a powerful reminder each time we record spiritual experiences and impressions in a journal and share them with family. One experience I recorded in my journal was on the day of the Seattle Washington Temple dedication. When I arrived, a large group of eager people was lined up waiting for the temple gates to open, hoping to get in. I, fortunately, had a special dedication ticket, which allowed me to enter immediately through a different door. The ticket was issued to me because my mom and I were selected to be in the choir that would sing in the celestial room during President Kimball's dedication. As I passed this long line of people, I couldn't help seeing the metaphorical significance of this moment, even as a teenager. They were all locked out without the particular pass I held. I sailed past them because of careful preparations beforehand. I thought about the line of ten virgins at the coming of the Lord's Supper, five wise and five foolish, and wanted at that moment to be ultimately counted among the wise, with my lamp full.

I guarded the dedication ticket in my journal along with my description of that visual impression. In the passing years, I forgot about this experience until much later when I found the ticket and the entry in my journal. It jogged my memory, and the feelings came flooding back. I was able to produce the ticket and use that experience in a family home evening lesson to share with my children.

Another token memorial can be the naming of children. Parents might name their child after a notable person in the scriptures, Church history, or family ancestry. Every day, these children carry with them a reminder of who they represent. We have followed that practice in our family. Recently, my sweet mother-in-law wrote an email to my husband. She reminded him of the scripture when Helaman spoke to his two sons, Nephi and Lehi. "Behold, my sons, I desire that ye should remember to keep the commandments of God; and I would that ye should declare unto the people these words. Behold, I have given unto you the names of our first parents who came out of the land of Jerusalem; and this I have done that when you remember your names ye may remember them; and when ye remember them ye may remember their words; and when ye remember their words ye may know how that it is said, and also written, that they were good. Therefore, my sons, I would that ye should do that which is good, that it may be said of you, and also written, even as it has been said and written of them" (Helaman 5:6–7). My mother-in-law wrote:

> Roland, you were named for two righteous men. Roland is your father's middle name. I don't know of a man who tries harder and more sincerely to keep the commandments of God and to follow in the footsteps of our Savior than your father does. He is worthy of your emulation in every way. And Henry is my father's name. What a privilege it is to bear the name of a Patriarch like your grandfather. We appreciate so much the way you serve your family and the Lord in every way you can. You are certainly carrying on the legacy of good works. We love you and appreciate your sacrifices!

The Church invests impressive amounts of money and resources to create places of memorial from Church history. My family and I have visited many of these places such as Martin's Cove, Nauvoo, and the Sacred Grove. These are sites that help us remember and hold onto the faith shown there. We too can establish visual reminders that tie our children to spiritual events.

Sometimes in sacrament meeting with children fighting and babies crying, we might wonder, "Why am I here?" Some parents have renamed Monday nights to "family home screaming" after some children expressed disagreements in a particularly vocal manner. Building memorials can seem hardly inspirational at times. Thinking of Joshua's example, we are reminded that each time we gather with our families, we are putting a stone in our living family altar.

We don't have to do anything dramatic or spectacular to establish symbols of faith. Over our kitchen door, we have a plaque engraved with the words:

> Fear not, for I have REDEEMED you; I have summoned you by name; you are mine.
>
> Isaiah 43:1

Parents may choose to give their child a meaningful memento on their baptismal date or create childhood photo albums and scrapbooks so they can relish memories again and again. When my parents returned from their mission, their adult children and their spouses presented them with a magnificent handmade quilt. It had large family photos printed on fabric on one side and handprints and names of all the grandchildren on the other. The quote from Isaiah 54:13 was the centerpiece: "And all thy children shall be taught of the Lord; and great shall be the peace of thy children." It was a memorial we built to honor their example of sacrificing to serve a mission to bless their family.

When my daughter Rachel was eleven years old, we went boating on a lake in Washington State at a family reunion. She was having fun being pulled on a tube behind the boat. A wave runner came too close to Rachel and hit her, and she sustained a concussion and deep gash on the side of her face. Miraculously, she avoided a fatal collision. There were many prayers and priesthood administrations. As terrible as it could have been, she did not experience any serious effects. At her hospital bedside, I told her that her life had been spared and that each day after that experience was a gift from Heavenly Father. What she did with her life would be her gift back to Him. To remember the occasion and spiritual impressions, I wrote these lines of testimony and gave them to her:

Miracle on the Water

Only a wrinkle left—
a scar of aging
long before you grow old.

Not yet twelve,
now wise beyond years,
knowing you were spared.

The divine brush left just
enough mark above your ear
to whisper, *He was there.*

Another illustration comes from a friend who took a hike with his father when he was a teenager. His father pointed out a tree that had grown sideways. He asked his son why he thought that tree was not vertical like other trees. My friend couldn't come up with an answer, so his dad said, "There was a heavy ice and snow pack that overwhelmed that tree when it was small and weak and kept it from growing upright. After a while, the tree couldn't straighten itself, and it became permanently altered to that position." His father then spoke of how sin can weigh us down and, if we don't unburden ourselves, can cripple our spirits. He took a picture of the tree, framed it, and put it in his son's bedroom. It made such a lasting impression that my friend still remembers it as an older father himself.

If my dad's briefcase can evoke such feelings in me, reflect on what other memorials we can create to remind our children of their testimony and faith. Continue building living memorials as a legacy for your children. A Monday family home evening, held consistency over the years, creates a memory no power can break. Rituals, such as gathering around the table for dinner, can lead to many positive physical, social, spiritual, and emotional outcomes. Elder Robert D. Hales asked,

> When we sit down at the dinner table, is our whole family there? I remember as a young man asking permission to play baseball through dinnertime. "Just put my meal in the oven," I said to my mother. She responded, "Robert, I really want you to take a break, come home, be with the family for dinner, and then you can go out and play baseball until dark." She taught all of us that where family meals are concerned, it's not the food but the family interaction that nourishes the soul. My mother taught that the greatest love we give is within our homes.[1]

In Joshua 4:16, the "ark of the covenant" is also called the "ark of the testimony." We, as parents, carry within us a testimony. "Not written with ink, but with the Spirit of the living God; not in tables of stone, but in the fleshy tables of the heart" (2 Corinthians 3:3). It isn't something tangible like my father's briefcase he carried every day, but when used often, a testimony can have an even more powerful and long-lasting effect on our children. Alma found that in stirring up others in remembrance and true conversion, he saw no other way than "bearing down in pure testimony" (Alma 4:19). How can we stand firm, like the ark-bearing priests confronting uncertain waters, and testify in front of and to our children? To be sure, it takes a leap of faith. Elder David A. Bednar stated,

> We also can become more diligent and concerned at home by bearing testimony to those whom we love about the things we know to be true by the witness of the Holy Ghost. The bearing of testimony need not be lengthy or eloquent. And we do not need to wait until the first Sunday of the month to declare our witness of things that are true. Within the walls of our own homes, we can and should bear pure testimony of the divinity and reality of the Father and the Son, of the great plan of happiness, and of the Restoration. . . . Our testimony of gospel truth should be reflected both in our words and in our deeds. And our testimonies are proclaimed and lived most powerfully in our own homes. Spouses, parents, and children should strive to overcome any hesitancy, reluctance, or embarrassment about bearing testimony. We should both create and look for opportunities to bear testimony of gospel truths—and live them.[2]

Contrast this counsel to what happened after Joshua died. Parents neglected to teach and testify to the next generation. "And there arose another generation after them, which knew not the Lord, nor yet the works which he had done for Israel" (Judges 2:10). Elder Bednar offered parents the specific counsel of bearing spontaneous testimony in natural settings for a meaningful personal connection. He explained, "Parents should be vigilant and spiritually attentive to spontaneously occurring opportunities to bear testimony to their children. Such occasions need not be programmed, scheduled, or scripted. In fact, the less regimented such testimony sharing is, the greater the likelihood for edification and lasting impact."[3]

My neighbor put this principle into practice when his daughter tried out and made the high school competitive ballroom dance team. He prayed many times for her to make it, in spite of the fact that she was less experienced than the other participants. When the family heard she had made the team, they were amazed. He knelt down in the privacy of his bedroom and thanked his Heavenly Father for this blessing. He felt the strong impression: "Testify to your daughter." He wondered how to do this naturally and spontaneously. It would have felt awkward to approach her at that moment and say, "I witness to you . . ." so he waited for the right moment.

Soon after, his daughter came into his office and started talking animatedly about the ballroom team. Within their conversation, he added gently, "I want you to know that Heavenly Father has blessed you with this opportunity and the talent to do so well. He has made this miracle happen so you can bless others on the team. Through your righteous influence, the entire team will be united and blessed." She was visibly moved and the impact of that moment was incalculable to them both. That spiritual impression was realized during the school year. She was instrumental in sharing the light of the gospel not only to the team but also to the families of the dancers, the faculty, and the student body.

As we bear testimony in naturally occurring settings, we can follow Elder Bednar's advice that "a testimony need not always begin with the phrase 'I bear you my testimony.' Our witness can be declared as simply as 'I know I was blessed with inspiration at work today' or 'The truth in this scripture always has been a powerful source of direction for me.'"[4] Other examples might be:

- "That experience reminds me of how good the Lord is to our family because . . ."

- "When I did what was right, I felt . . ."

- "I was certainly blessed when . . ."

- "When I was praying today, I felt the Holy Ghost direct me to call you."

- "Heavenly Father has blessed you with so many talents."

- "I love to look at nature and know how everything was created by a loving Heavenly Father for us to enjoy."

In the restored gospel, consistent reminders of our words and deeds help us retain a bright testimony. Isn't the sacrament a visual token we take in remembrance of Christ's sacrifice? In the Book of Mormon, Helaman advised, "Behold, my sons, I desire that ye should remember to keep the commandments of God. . . . O remember, remember my sons, the words which King Benjamin spake unto his people; yea, remember that there is no other way nor means whereby man can be saved, only through the atoning blood of Jesus Christ, who shall come; yea, remember that he cometh to redeem the world. . . . And now, my sons, remember, remember that it is upon the rock of our Redeemer, who is Christ, the Son of God, that ye must build your foundation . . ." (see Helaman 5:6, 9, 12).

How many "remembers" did you count? After Helaman spoke to his sons, "They did remember his words" (Helaman 5:14). Clearly, the key to righteousness is remembering!

Parenting principles from Joshua: Visual reminders are inextricably tied to remembering spiritual events. We can establish memorials for our children to hold onto as they develop their own beliefs. Parents should stand firm in bearing spontaneous testimony in natural settings. These will tie them to you and to the Lord, and these memorials will give them strength and the gift of remembering.

NOTES

1.   Robert D. Hales, "Our Duty to God: The Mission of Parents and Leaders to the Rising Generation," *Ensign,* May 2010, 95–96.

2.   David A. Bednar, "More Diligent and Concerned at Home," *Ensign,* November 2009, 18–19.

3.   David A. Bednar, "Watching with All Perseverance," *Ensign,* May 2010, 42.

4.   Bednar, "Watching with All Perseverance," 42.

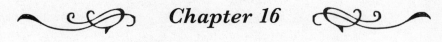

Chapter 16

THE PRODIGAL SON:
THE POWER OF LOVE

What do we do with our wayward child? This is a soul-cry of so many parents. As with all parenting processes, one answer will not fit all cases. Each child is different as are the promptings of the Spirit for how to best approach individual needs. This chapter is dedicated to fundamental gospel principles to guide our decisions as we seek for specific answers to prayers. Christ taught in parables so that universal truths could be applied to each listener. We begin with the exemplary parable of the prodigal son.

A man had two sons, one faithful and one foolish. The younger demanded his inheritance early to live a riotous existence in a distant land, disgracing his family. He eventually squandered all he had been given. Moreover, this foolish youth continued rebelling as he sunk to the depths of circumstances by feeding swine that ate better than he. Some of today's parents can identify with the father of this young man, having experienced a similar betrayal and disappointment from their own children.

For some undetermined period, the prodigal son stayed in the pig sty, unable (or unwilling) to pull himself out of spiritual darkness and despair. We often rush past this episode in the story. Many rebellious youth are forced to face a low point before they can face themselves and those they have turned from. The narration continues, "And when he came to himself . . ." (Luke 15:17). But let's pause here for a moment. How long did it take him—envying pigs, covered with mud and self-loathing—to come to himself? We do not know. There is no timetable given. Christ told the story so masterfully that we are able to apply it to any parental situation. Some children return home quickly; some take much longer. However, the message is clear: through the process of time, there is hope in eventual repentance and reconciliation if they were brought up in the light of the gospel. *Righteous parents provide the contrast so their children know the way back to the light from the darkness.*

Such was the case with this prodigal. It was only when he remembered his privileged former life that he realized his current depraved ways. He knew his father's servants ate better than the slop he was driven to eat. The wayward son began to sorrow for the evil he had done and vowed to repent before his father. "And he arose, and came to his father. But when he was yet a great way off, his father saw him, and had compassion, and ran, and fell on his neck, and kissed him" (Luke 15:20). Elder Jeffrey R. Holland spoke of this reunion: "He determined to find his way home, hoping to be accepted at least as a servant in his father's household. The tender image of this boy's anxious, faithful father running to meet him and showering him with kisses is one of the most moving and compassionate scenes in all of holy writ. It tells every child of God, wayward or otherwise, how much God wants us back in the protection of His arms."[1]

Here is an enduring image for any parent: the father standing at the crossroads, day after day, waiting for his son to return. This diligent, watchful parent was first to see his son while he was "a great way off" because his eyes never failed to scan the horizon. We too must look beyond our suffering, to rise up each day and embrace the message of hope. Elder Dieter F. Uchdorf stated, "Hope . . . is like the beam of sunlight rising up and above the horizon of our present circumstances. It pierces the darkness with a brilliant dawn. It encourages and inspires us to place our trust in the loving care of an eternal Heavenly Father, who has prepared a way for those who seek for eternal truth in a world of relativism, confusion, and of fear."[2]

The image of Christ as the Good Shepherd is one of the most cherished among Christians. Christ illustrated in this parable that a true shepherd will leave the ninety and nine to seek tirelessly for a lost lamb (see Luke 15:1–7). There are many lost sheep in families today, and after our best efforts, some still wander. How grateful we are that the eye of the Good Shepherd knows where to find a lost child and whose hand knows how to beckon them back.

"You possibly can't do this alone," reassured Elder Jeffrey R. Holland,

but you *do* have help. The Master of Heaven and Earth is there to bless you—He who resolutely goes after the lost sheep, sweeps thoroughly to find the lost coin, waits everlastingly for the return of the prodigal son. Yours is the work of salvation, and therefore you will be magnified, compensated, made more than you are and better than you have ever been as you try to make honest effort, however feeble you may sometimes feel that to be.[3]

The partnership of earthly parent and Shepherd of all creation elevates our understanding of eternal principles and opportunity to practice them with His help. Elder Robert D. Hales added his witness:

To parents and families throughout the world, I testify that the Lord Jesus Christ is mighty to save. He is the Healer, the Redeemer, the rescuing Shepherd who will leave the ninety and nine to find the one. If we are seeking the salvation of special 'ones' in our own families, I bear testimony that they are within His reach. We assist Him in reaching them by faithfully living the gospel, being sealed in the temple, and living true to the covenants we make there.[4]

Once the repentant prodigal son confessed his sins, the father offered forgiveness freely, with no reservations. The father in this parable typifies our perfect Father. Isaiah observed the parallel between these two: "Let the wicked forsake his way, and the unrighteous man his thoughts: and let him return unto the Lord, and he will have mercy upon him; and to our God, for he will *abundantly pardon*" (Isaiah 55:7; emphasis added).

In the parable of the prodigal son, elaborated Elder Robert D. Hales, we find a powerful lesson for families and especially parents. After the younger son "came to himself," he decided to go home.

How did he know his father wouldn't reject him? Because he knew his father. Through the inevitable misunderstandings, conflicts, and follies of the son's youth, I can visualize his father being there with an understanding and compassionate heart, a soft answer, a listening ear, and a forgiving embrace. I can also imagine his son knowing he could come home because he knew the kind of home that was awaiting him. For the scriptures say, "When he was yet a great way off, his father saw him, and had compassion, and ran, and fell on his neck, and kissed him" [Luke 15:20].

I testify that our Heavenly Father leaves the door open. I also testify that it is never too late to open the door between us and our children with simple words such as "I love you," "I am sorry," and "Please forgive me." We can begin now to create a home they will want to return to—not only now but in the eternities.[5]

The prodigal's parent spared nothing in celebration of his son's return. The son was clothed in the best robes, given a ring of power, shoes for his feet, and the grandest family feast. These are metaphors of the riches and blessings promised to those who are endowed in the temple and sealed under the new and everlasting covenant of marriage.

The story of the prodigal is about turning and returning—turning away from sin and turning toward his father and his God. Elijah restored the keys of the sealing power to Joseph Smith in the Kirtland Temple. Elijah promised that "he shall plant in the hearts of the children the promises made to the fathers, and the hearts of the children shall turn to their fathers" (D&C 2:2). What are the promises made to fathers? Families can be sealed together for eternity. In consequence, Elijah prophesied that children sealed under the covenant will remember those promises and their hearts will turn to their fathers. Here is a promise from Lorenzo Snow to parents who raise their children in righteousness and await the promised blessings according to their child's agency and God's timetable:

> God has fulfilled His promises to us, and our prospects are grand and glorious. Yes, in the next life we will have . . . our sons and daughters. If we do not get them all at once, we will have them some time. . . . You that are mourning about your children straying away will have your sons and your daughters. If you succeed in passing through these trials and afflictions and receive a resurrection, you will, by the power of the Priesthood, work and labor, as the Son of God has, until you get all your sons and daughters in the path of exaltation and glory. This is just as sure as that the sun rose this morning over yonder mountains. Therefore, mourn not because all your sons and daughters do not follow in the path that you have marked out to them, or give heed to your counsels. Inasmuch as we succeed in securing eternal glory, and stand as saviors, and as kings and priests to our God, we will save our posterity.[6]

While the parable of the prodigal son gives us hope, the scriptures also provide assurances of real families with repentant sons and steadfast mothers and fathers. In the book of Mosiah in the Book of Mormon, we read of two contemporaries and friends, Mosiah and Alma. These men were faithful fathers who demonstrated what love can do. Both suffered the trial, pain, and humiliation of having sons who were the "very vilest of sinners" (Mosiah 28:4). This must have been especially grievous as they were in high positions and esteemed by the people, being the king and high priest, yet their sons went about actively to destroy the Church.

How long these faithful fathers prayed for their sons, we do not know. What they did to exhort and influence their wayward children is not written. What we do know, however, is that these fathers never gave up and continued to pray and love their sons. Their examples teach us when there is nothing left to do, we can still *pray for*, have *faith in*, and *love* our children. These are three of the strongest principles when we desire to maintain some degree of influence over children lost in the midst of spiritual darkness.

As a result of prayer, Alma eventually called down the powers of heaven. We read that an angel was compelled to intervene and stop Alma the Younger from further damaging the Church. The angel appeared before him and the sons of Mosiah and said, "Behold, the Lord hath heard the prayers . . . of his servant, Alma, who is thy father; for he has prayed with much faith concerning thee that thou mightest be brought to the knowledge of the truth; therefore, for this purpose have I come to convince thee of the power and authority of God, that the prayers of his servants might be answered according to their faith" (Mosiah 27:14). From that moment, these sons changed dramatically. They became unshakable in their faith in God and instrumental in preaching the gospel to wayward Nephites.

Moroni explained how this angelic appearance was in accordance to the laws of heaven: "And because he hath done this, my beloved brethren, have miracles ceased? Behold I say unto you, Nay; neither have angels ceased to minister unto the children of men. For behold, they are subject unto him, to minister according to the word of his command, showing themselves unto them of strong faith and a firm mind" (Moroni 7:29–30).

My dear neighbors raised a son who gave them rebellion and heartache. After years of prayer, worry, fasting, and faith, he continued to spiral downward. Finally, this humble couple had an impression to pray to know the Lord's will. What was *His* plan to save their son? Through this, they learned *what* to pray for: a friend for him. From then on, they knew how the Lord needed to bless their son. They prayed for a friend, and soon after, one came into their son's life that changed him. These faithful parents used the same principles as Alma and King Mosiah. Their prayers may not have sent a celestial messenger to their wayward son, but they gave him instead an earthly angel to minister to his specific needs. In short, a miracle.

If praying for our children is necessary, praying for ourselves is essential if we are to develop the pure love of Christ. When a child has severely disappointed or hurt us, it might be difficult to forgive or to love him or her. Nevertheless, our pain can gain us a new perceptive on the tender mercies of our Father in Heaven. How else can we practice forgiveness if we have not been wronged? How can we develop charity unless we are able to exercise faith and hope? Elder Lynn G. Robbins advised,

> A sweet and obedient child will enroll a father or mother only in Parenting 101. If you are blessed with a child who tests your patience to the nth degree, you will be enrolled in Parenting 505. Rather than wonder what you might have done wrong in the premortal life to be so deserving, you might consider the more challenging child a blessing and opportunity to become more godlike yourself. With which child will your patience, long-suffering, and other Christlike virtues most likely be tested, developed, and refined? Could it be possible that you need this child as much as this child needs you?[7]

Moroni lived at a time when the Nephites were extremely depraved and eventually destroyed by the Lamanites. Surely he had many experiences with seemingly unlovable people. In a poignant moment, he wrote of his utter aloneness in a land of wickedness: "My father hath been slain in battle, and all my kinsfolk, and I have not friends nor whither to go; and how long the Lord will suffer that I may live I know not. . . . And behold also, the Lamanites are at war one with another; and the whole face of this land is one continual round of murder and bloodshed" (Mormon 8:5, 8). I can always feel the pathos in this passage.

Yet, in subsequent verses, Moroni wrote to his posterity of charity—the pure love of Christ. "Wherefore, my beloved brethren, pray unto the Father with all the energy of heart, that ye may be filled with this love, which he hath bestowed upon all who are true followers of his Son, Jesus Christ; that ye may become the sons of God; that when he shall appear we shall be like him, for we shall see him as he is; that we may have this hope; that we may be purified even as he is pure" (Moroni 7:48). Moroni expressed this charity toward the very people who wronged him the most—those who killed his father, family, and friends, who left him alone to flee for his life. He affirmed, "I am filled with charity, which is everlasting love; wherefore, all children are alike unto me; wherefore, I love little children with a perfect love" (Moroni 8:17).

When we have a child who tests our ability to love, Moroni taught us to pray to be filled with love. If we plead for the grace of Christ, our deficiencies can be made strong. His enabling Atonement makes up for our inadequacies. Our faltering love can be revived. My friend had a stubborn, strong-willed son who tested both parents' patience. He was difficult to raise. From a young age, it was either his way or the highway. My friend kept praying for him to change but saw little improvement over the years. One day, she realized that instead of trying to change him, she needed a change in her own heart. So she prayed to view him differently. It was almost immediate. Instead of his problems, she saw potential. She rejoiced in his uniqueness. She gained perspective and patience unimagined before. Since that moment, whenever she thinks about him, even when he exercises his willfulness, she just smiles. Today that same stubborn, strong-willed young man is serving as a missionary, passionate about the work and people he serves. I know of no stronger attachment than between this mother and son.

Elder James E. Faust, with his wise years of perspective, reassured us: "A wonderful couple I knew in my youth had a son who was rebellious and estranged himself from their family. But in their later years, he reconciled with them and was the most caring and solicitous of all their children. As we get older, the pull from our parents and grandparents on the other side of the veil becomes stronger."[8] Doctrine and Covenants section 50 also speaks of this redemptive power:

> But blessed are they who are faithful and endure, whether in life or in death, for they shall inherit eternal life.
>
> But wo unto them that are deceivers and hypocrites, for, thus saith the Lord, I will bring them to judgment.
>
> Behold, verily I say unto you, there are hypocrites among you, who have deceived some, which has given the adversary power; but behold *such shall be reclaimed.* (vv. 5–7; emphasis added)

When my eldest son was eight, he asked me a question he had discussed that day in a science unit at school. "What is the most powerful force on earth?" I answered instinctively, "Love." "No," he responded. "Something you can see." So I thought for a moment and said, "Water." "Right," he answered, and we talked about the properties of water and how great a force can be channeled to generate electricity or how destructive it can be in a hurricane. However, if you were to ask me the same question today, I would say, "Love, because you *can* see it." It is manifest in the unremitting outstretched arms of a parent whose child refuses the embrace. It is manifest in a parent whose eyes are ever lifted to the crossroads for a sign of a returning prodigal. It is found in the words, "Of course I forgive you. Will you forgive me?" Love is what parenting with spiritual power is about.

Parenting principles from the prodigal son: We are on earth to practice godlike attributes so we can exercise them eternally as parents. One of the most difficult yet godly traits is to extend the arms of mercy, as Christ does for us, to our wayward children. We need to pray to be filled with charity for all men. There is hope in the redemptive power of Christ for rebellious children. Christ is the Good Shepherd who seeks after His lost sheep. We need to *pray for*, have *faith in*, and *love* these special children. If we provide the light of the gospel while they are young, it will provide a contrast to the dark paths they might choose, and help them find their way back home.

NOTES

1. Jeffrey R. Holland, "The Other Prodigal," *Ensign*, May 2002, 62.

2. Dieter F. Uchdorf, "The Infinite Power of Hope," *Ensign*, November 2008, 22.

3. Jeffrey R. Holland, "Because She is a Mother," *Ensign*, May 1997, 36–37.

4. Robert D. Hales, "With All the Feelings of a Tender Parent: A Message of Hope to Families," *Ensign*, May 2004, 91.

5. Hales, "With All the Feelings of a Tender Parent," 90.

6. Lorenzo Snow, as cited by David E. Sorensen, "The Doctrine of Temple Work," *Ensign*, October 2003, 63; original quote in *Millennial Star*, January 22, 1894, 51–52.

7. Lynn G. Robbins, "What Manner of Men and Women Ought Ye to Be?" *Ensign*, May 2011, 104.

8. James E. Faust, "Dear Are the Sheep That Have Wandered," *Ensign*, May 2003, 67.

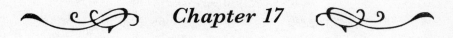

Chapter 17

MOSES AND THE PASSOVER: THE POWER OF CONNECTIONS TO CHRIST

I took a seven-year-old boy who came from a less-active family to sacrament meeting. It was his first time there. Before the sacrament was administered, I tried to explain what the bread and water symbolized, but in those brief moments, I could tell the real meaning was lost on him. After he took a small piece of bread and swallowed it, he turned to me and said, "I don't think that's going to be *near* enough."

How can parents teach the symbolic nature of the gospel to their children? How can we turn abstract ideas into concrete concepts that even young children can grasp and remember? Consider the parenting counsel of Moses in this matter. While the children of Israel were in bondage to the Egyptians, the Lord sent various plagues to show forth His divine power and afflict the Egyptians that His people might be freed. Before the final plague, Moses instructed the Israelites to kill a firstborn lamb without blemish and strike the doorposts with its blood as a covenant sign of the Passover. "For the Lord will pass through to smite the Egyptians; and when he seeth the blood upon the lintel, and on the two side posts, the Lord will pass over the door, and will not suffer the destroyer to come in unto your homes to smite you. And ye shall observe this thing for an ordinance to thee and to thy sons forever" (Exodus 12:23–24).

"And it shall come to pass," Moses continued, "when your children shall say unto you, What mean ye by this service? That ye shall say, It is the sacrifice of the Lord's passover, who passed over the houses of the children of Israel in Egypt, when he smote the Egyptians, and delivered our houses" (Exodus 12:26–27). In response to this covenant, the people bowed their heads and worshipped and did as they were commanded. Moses gave them the new covenant and commanded them to teach it to their children.

Moses foresaw that their children might not understand the spiritual meaning behind the ritualistic Mosaic laws. He anticipated their wonderment at why they were doing these things ("What mean ye by this service?"). His instructions included using Christ as the central figure. Similarly, we make covenants in the restored Church that have symbolic meaning. As Moses instructed his people, we must teach the connection between symbols and Christ to the rising generation. It is imperative to teach how "all things which have been given of God from the beginning of the world, unto man, are the typifying of [Christ]" (2 Nephi 11:4).

Adam and Eve knew not why they were told to offer "the firstlings of their flocks for an offering unto the Lord" (Moses 5:5). They did it out of obedience, but they did not understand the spiritual significance. In time, God sent an angel to reveal the symbolism of animal sacrifice. He explained, "This thing is a similitude of the sacrifice of the Only Begotten of the Father, which is full of grace and truth. Wherefore, thou shalt do all that thou doest in the name of the Son and thou shalt repent and call upon God in the name of the Son forevermore" (Moses 5:7–8). That same day, the Holy Ghost fell upon Adam and bore witness to the truth of all things. Do you want to invite the Spirit to testify of truth to your child? Teach the meaning of gospel symbols and their foundation in Christ.

We often assume our children know what we know because they do what we do. They go through the motions of church worship and gospel living but may not understand the purpose. Such was the case of my friend. She encouraged her children to say their personal prayers every night. Even her five-year-old committed to praying by his bedside. He came up to her one night and said proudly, "Mom, I'm remembering to pray by myself." She praised him and watched him that evening. Sure enough, he was kneeling by his bed, reverently bowing in the act of prayer. After he got up, she tucked him in bed and praised him again. He beamed and agreed he was doing a good job. As an afterthought, she asked him,

"So what kinds of things are you praying for?" He looked puzzled. "You mean, you're supposed to be saying something?"

Latter-day Saint families perpetuate a pattern of rituals. Do our children ever wonder why we are offered bread and water every Sunday, why baptism involves going underwater, or what temples are for? As they grow into youth, do they question the importance of keeping the Sabbath day or why they must be married in a temple? It is necessary to clarify the symbolic nature of our covenants so our children see the spiritual meaning behind them. The temple is rich with symbols. Teach familiarity with symbolism found in our world and Church so the temple becomes an extension of that prior knowledge when your son or daughter receives his or her ordinances. This requires many teachings over time, as children's cognitive abilities evolve. By explaining how each covenant points to Christ and His Atonement and their relationship to Him, they can feel safety, power, and joy in their lives. The Holy Ghost testifies of truth. Whenever truth is taught by a parent, He will be there to bring peace.

We can translate gospel concepts to make them understandable, Christ-centered, and personal for our children. Parents and teachers can approach this as they teach in concrete, tangible terms that can be applied and teach the "whys" of the gospel by focusing on doctrine rather than just behavior (see also chapter 2).

When my children were younger, I wanted to teach the importance of listening to the Holy Ghost, a being they cannot see. We drove up the canyon and turned off on an exit that led to a nearby river. We sat by the river and the few trees that sheltered the bank. There they were able to hear my lesson on the Holy Ghost in a restful, quiet atmosphere. When we were done, we took a few steps away from the bank and immediately were assaulted by the tumult of traffic. Although the river was still near, its quiet sound was drowned by the distant but glaring noise. The contrast was stark. I told them that stepping into the noise and confusion of the world is sometimes like that—we lose the ability to hear the quiet whisperings of the Spirit. Nature has a way of teaching natural connections to the gospel if we take advantage.

Especially young children have difficulty understanding abstract concepts and symbolic thinking. They have not yet developed formal abilities of higher reasoning. Ask a young child why we fast, and you might get the answer: "To get really hungry." Abstract ideas can be packaged into concrete. When speaking about doctrine such as "reverence," "faith," "baptism," and "sacrament," parents should search for ways to continually teach the "whys" in age-appropriate terms and integrate concrete ideas. Consider the following differences in teaching reverence at church:

Abstract: "Please be reverent. Keep your arms folded and mouth quiet."

Concrete: "Remember this is Heavenly Father's house. We show respect for Him by walking with quiet feet down the hall. It helps to look at the pictures on the walls and think about His son, Jesus Christ."

The first example used seemingly disparate ideas (reverence = holding still). We can be sitting still but not have our hearts and minds centered on Christ. The second connected reverence to its true antecedent: respect for and reflection on Jesus Christ. The abstract addressed only the outward behaviors with no explanation; the concrete gave a purpose and meaning so that quiet behaviors would likely follow. This reminds me of a story I once heard of a father who went to check on his daughter and friends playing together. As he approached the bedroom, he saw his daughter standing on a chair with her three friends dolefully sitting below. She had her arms folded and her face pinched in stern chastisement. The father called her out and asked her what she was doing. She said, "We're playing church and how to be reverent." He asked her how they played "reverent." She responded, "Well you fold your arms, scrunch up your face, and hurt. But I have to go back in the bedroom because it's my turn to shush the other kids." Is that what "reverence" means to children from our outward appearance?

Christ, our Master Teacher, taught by comparing abstract concepts to everyday tangible objects. His new followers were young in their understanding of gospel principles, much like children. He knew how metaphors, parables, and other comparative symbolism can help a young learner understand, apply, and retain principles. If the learner was able to attach a teaching to something concrete, every time he saw that symbol he would be reminded of the spiritual meaning, make personal connections, and gain an ever-deepening understanding with his own experience and gospel maturity. These are some of the abstract-to-concrete connections Christ used:

- Faith = Mustard seed
- Sin = Millstone around neck

- Types of hearers = Four kinds of soil

- Just and unjust = Wheat and tares or sheep and goats

- New law and Mosaic law = New wine in old bottles

- Missionary work = Fishers of men

- Body = Temple

- Good works = Light on a hill

- The Messiah = The Bread of Life, the Living Water, the Good Shepherd, the Rock

- Testimony = Oil lamp

- Hypocrisy = Whitened sepulchers

Standing alone, these objects have little doctrinal meaning. But parents and teachers who make skillful connections for children have a powerful teaching tool.

Years ago, I struggled to teach a Young Women class about the importance of a temple marriage. Only a few had been inside to do baptisms or had a goal of marrying in the temple. The rest were uncommitted to making those covenants and living the lifestyle required. Even these young ladies had difficulty internalizing the abstract ideals of a place they had never been. As I prayed and prepared the lesson on temple marriage, I searched to know how I could teach it in the way the Savior taught, using everyday tangible objects to make spiritual connections to Christ. I still didn't have an answer by Sunday and felt the lesson was incomplete.

As I drove to church, I kept a prayer in my heart for the girls to hold onto these sacred, spiritual concepts in a very real way. As I got out of the car, I noticed a single orange rolling around the floor. It must have escaped the grocery sack earlier that week . . . perhaps with the aid of a heavenly hand! I knew I needed to use it and instantly knew how.

During the lesson, I showed the young ladies the orange and told them to imagine they had never seen or tasted one before. What did they guess it would be like inside? How would it taste? We had a productive and meaningful discussion. I told them it was like the temple. I had been inside. I had tasted of the sweet spirit. I testified of how wondrous it was and how I wanted to share it with others. I slowly peeled away the orange rind and showed them—as if for their first time—an amazing orange. They smelled the aroma.

We discussed how Heavenly Father created oranges in such a way that you can easily share one with many people. If they had never seen the inside before, how would they know all it contained? It had so many sections, so many perfectly organized parts. I gave a section to each of the girls and told them to eat it, as if for the first time. What did it taste like? How did it make them feel? I shared my testimony of the temple, its perfect organization of families, its sweet spirit, its beauty. I told them they needed to exercise faith that like this orange, there is something extraordinary inside the Lord's house and it was worth everything to be married there.

Most of the objects employed by Christ were in the context of parables and storytelling. When we tell stories or give personal examples, we are really giving the listener something to hold on to. We imagine the story in our minds and remember it for a long time. We naturally respond with, "Oh, I had something similar happen to me." They are easy to retell. The images are vivid. When your family has finished watching general conference, what do your children (or you) remember? Most likely the stories. They are the backdrop for painting our own life's experiences.

Likening stories and events from the scriptures to our own lives can lead to personal reflections and understanding of principles. Elder Robert D. Hales shared how he used application from his own parenting experience:

> Several years ago I was teaching our young son about the life and experiences of the brother of Jared. Although the story was very interesting, he was not engaged. I then asked what the story meant to him personally. It means so much when we ask our children, "What does it mean to you?" He said, "You know, it's not that different from what Joseph Smith did in the grove when he prayed and got an answer."
>
> I said, "You're about Joseph's age. Do you think a prayer like his would be helpful to you?" Suddenly, we weren't talking about a long-ago story in a faraway land. We were talking about our son—about his life, his needs, and the way prayer could help him.
>
> As parents, we have the responsibility to help our children to "liken all scriptures [indeed, every part of the gospel of Jesus Christ] unto us [and unto our children] . . . for [the] profit and learning [of our families]" (1 Nephi 19:23).
>
> Are we likening all of our children's gospel experiences to the real needs in their lives? Are we teaching them about the gift of the Holy Ghost, repentance, the Atonement, the sacrament, and the blessing of sacrament meeting as they meet the challenges in their lives? There is not enough time in formal meetings to teach our children everything

they need to know. Therefore, we must *take advantage of everyday teaching moments.*[1]

Let us examine other examples of how to teach concepts effectively like Moses outlined. Also keep in mind that doctrine, rather than discussion of behavior, changes behavior more effectively. The following contrasts behavior-only statements with doctrinally based statements:

Behavior: "Sit up in your chair so you won't fall over or bother your neighbor."

Doctrine: "We sit quietly in our chairs so one day you will be ready to go to the temple, where everyone sits quietly to show respect and love for Heavenly Father's house."

Behavior: "No way are you going to wear a tattoo. And one ear piercing is enough. Don't be so foolish to follow the crowd and do something you'll regret later."

Doctrine: "Our bodies are God-given and sacred. I know you would never deface the walls of the temple. We keep our bodies clean on the outside, like a temple, to remind us to keep the inside clean as well. You will be blessed to be worthy to enter the temple one day."

Primary songs are especially useful in teaching Christ-centered doctrine in simple yet elegant language. Their musical messages should vivify our lives. I remember singing the following primary song at the top of my lungs as a child as I walked to and from an afterschool class. It helped me imagine, in concrete and beautiful imagery, the idea of the Second Coming:

> *I wonder, when he comes again, will herald angels sing?*
> *Will earth be white with drifted snow, or will the world know spring?*
> *I wonder if one star will shine far brighter than the rest;*
> *Will daylight stay the whole night through? Will songbirds leave their nests?*
>
> *I'm sure he'll call his little ones together round his knee,*
> *Because he said in days gone by, "Suffer them to come to me."*[2]

The next primary song compares a seed growing to faith. Using metaphors like this can be very helpful in converting abstract ideas to concrete:

Faith is knowing the sun will rise, lighting each new day.

Faith is knowing the Lord will hear my prayers each time I pray.

Faith is like a little seed; if planted it will grow.

Faith is swelling within my heart, when I do right I know.[3]

Finally, I love this primary song that teaches the "whys" of reverence.

It shouldn't be hard to sit very still and think about Jesus, his cross on the hill,

And all that he suffered and did for me; it shouldn't be hard to sit quietly,

It shouldn't be hard, even though I am small, to think about Jesus, not hard at all

I think of the miles he walked in the dust, and children he helped to love and to trust;

It shouldn't be hard to sit tall in my seat, to listen politely, to quiet my feet,

It shouldn't be hard, even though I am small, to think about Jesus, not hard at all.[4]

To summarize this chapter, consider the scenario of family scripture study using the principles we have discussed: 1) Teach the "whys" of the gospel through doctrine rather than focusing solely on behavior; 2) Teach connections to Christ in concrete, tangible terms that can be applied.

1. Scatter a few pictures from the LDS Gospel Art Kit on the floor. Ask the children to listen as you read the scriptures and pick out which one of the pictures you are reading about. Hold up that picture and share a similar story from your life.

2. After reading a scripture story, ask, *"Has something like this happened to you where you felt _____ (worried/alone/grateful/obedient)?"* For example, after reading about Moroni wandering alone, surrounded by wickedness, you could ask a teenager, *"Do you ever feel the same way as you walk the halls of high school? Is it hard to stand up for righteousness? Why do you think Moroni was so steadfast in his virtue? Where do you think Moroni turned for strength? Where do you turn for strength?"* Bear testimony of

application—they will find answers to problems in the scriptures.

3. Set an object down in front of the family (for example, a container of salt) that will be mentioned in a verse you will read. *"Raise your hand when you hear the scriptures talking about this. What does it mean? What does it teach us of Christ?"*

4. After reading a passage, ask, *"How can we be more like _____ (Alma/Paul/Moses)?"* Or, for example, *"If you were one of the sons of Mosiah and you were stopped by an angel, what would you think? How would you change your life?"*

5. After reading a relevant passage, ask, *"What attribute does this writer demonstrate by his actions and words?* (Charity, faith, etc.) *How did Christ show that attribute during his ministry? Who do you know that is like this writer? Why are they that way? How can we be more like them?"*

6. When reading a particular passage in the Book of Mormon, ask, *"Why do you think this was included in the translated section of the Book of Mormon? How are people today like those in the scriptures?"*

7. When reading verses from a firsthand speaker, ask, *"Who is speaking on this page and who is he talking to? Where was he or she living and what do you think were his or her circumstances? Are they anything like yours?"* Compare and contrast.

8. If your family is studying and/or memorizing a particular scripture, hang it up all week with a picture that connects it to the principles taught. Have family members focus on one way to improve living that principle during the week. Tell them to imagine as if Christ were by their side in all decisions they make.

9. Summarize a scriptural passage in one sentence (that is, make up your own chapter headings). Or, before you read a chapter, ask the kids to be thinking while you read what title they would give the chapter, as if it were a book.

10. Have children draw out a slip of paper with a question (one that an investigator would ask) and ask where they would find the answer. Search by topic and use cross-section footnote references. I've done this as a literal role play with nametags my kids wore ("Investigator," "Missionary," and "Missionary Companion") and questions I gave the investigator to ask.

Challenge them to tie any question about the gospel to the reality of Christ.

11. Silently read a passage and have each family member ask a question at the end. Or ask younger children to read a passage and older kids to think of a question at the end. Discuss the answer.

12. Write a letter of encouragement to a persecuted scripture character, like the prophet Abinadi after they bind him and sentence him to death or Job while he is suffering his trials.

13. Have one child pretend to be a reporter and interview another child who pretends to be a scriptural character, like Joseph in Egypt while imprisoned after two years or the Apostle Paul marooned for three months on the isle of Malta. Talk about heroes and who is their hero (or heroine). If they could go back in time, what questions would they ask their hero?

14. Have children go on a scriptural treasure hunt. Place items to find and have them see how they relate to particular passages. Or have children find random objects throughout the house and bring them back. Go on a scripture hunt for passages that could relate to one of those objects (use the Bible Dictionary, Index, or Topical Guide or do a search for that word on lds.org on the "Scriptures" page). Leave the objects out with the scripture written next to them the next week.

15. Read a conference talk and ask, *"How do the living prophets and apostles help us live happier lives? What are they teaching us in this talk? If they shared a story, what was it?* (many children enjoy drawing a picture of the story). *What would our lives be like if we disobeyed their counsel?"* Read about the backgrounds of our general Church leaders (the Church's website has a chart of our General Authorities and their biographies).

16. When appropriate, substitute a child's name instead of the name mentioned in the scripture. Testify how their Heavenly Father and Jesus love us and commanded the prophets to write the scriptures so we can have their words today to be a personal guide.

17. After reading the scriptures, have the children write a response in their personal journals regarding how they feel about what they read and what they will do to improve their lives. If they are new to this, share an example of what you have written and goals you have set.

18. Have a few dress ups available for younger children to put on and

act out as you read, or re-tell a story from the scriptures. Next, show a picture of a person they know and tell how they have demonstrated the same attributes in their life. If it is an ancestor, talk about how Christ made it possible for us to be sealed as families. Search out information with older children and adolescents about ancestors who have not had their temple work done and get their name ready for the ordinances of salvation. Do the temple work as a family if possible.

19. When reading particularly difficult passages, or coming across unfamiliar words, insert understandable words or summaries. For example, you might be reading Romans 12:2: "And be not conformed to this world: but be ye transformed by the renewing of your mind, that ye may prove what is that good and acceptable, and perfect, will of God." After reading it, go through and reword it with something like, "Don't do what is worldly, or follow bad examples, but try to be a better person and what God wants us to be." Older children can often be the "translators."

20. Look for oft-repeated words in the scriptures, (like "seed" in Alma 32 or "Blessed" in the Beatitudes or "And thus we see . . ." in the Book of Mormon) and highlight key words. Ask, *Why are these words so important that they are repeated so many times?"*

Parenting principles from Moses: We should never assume our children understand gospel principles they enact every day. Teach how all things have a connection to Christ and their relationship to Him. All things should be likened to our lives and our children's lives for their profit and understanding. Primary songs are often doctrine taught in concrete, age-appropriate terms that will help us convey the gospel to young children. Two approaches to teaching young children are to emphasize the "whys" of the gospel through doctrine and to teach connections to Christ in concrete, tangible terms.

NOTES

1. Robert D. Hales, "With All the Feelings of a Tender Parent: A Message of Hope to Families," *Ensign,* May 2004, 90.

2. "When He Comes Again," *Children's Songbook,* 82–83.

3. "Faith," *Children's Songbook,* 96–97.

4. "To Think About Jesus," *Children's Songbook,* 71.

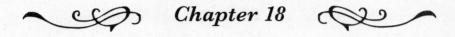

Chapter 18

RUTH AND MOSES: THE POWER OF HONORING PARENTS

Ruth is a noble figure and one of few women whose name titles a book in the Old Testament. Her life is evidence of the blessing parents receive through continued relations with their own aging parents and in-laws while raising their own children. Tragically, her mother-in-law, Naomi, lost her husband to an early death. Then adding to their sorrow, Ruth's husband and his brother both died. This left Ruth, her sister-in-law, and her mother-in-law destitute, without kinsmen to care for them. Naomi bade her two daughters-in-law, Ruth and Orpah, to return to their own homes and seek new husbands. Orpah eventually complied, but Ruth expressed these beautiful and cherished words: "Intreat me not to leave thee, or to return from following after thee: for whither thou goest, I will go; and where thou lodgest, I will lodge: thy people shall be my people, and thy God my God" (Ruth 1:16). Ruth followed her mother-in-law to a foreign land and was loyal to her throughout her life.

I have often wondered the meaning of the commandment, "Honour thy father and thy mother: that thy days may be long upon the land which the Lord thy God shall giveth thee" (Exodus 20:12). It is a commandment with a blessing. *Honor* and *live*. How are those two words related? In the case of Ruth, she followed her mother-in-law's careful instructions according to custom and sought Naomi's kinsman, Boaz, as a husband and protector. These customs might have seemed strange indeed to the Moabitess

Ruth, but she did as she was instructed and Boaz agreed to take her to wife.

Ruth and Boaz were blessed and prospered with posterity, which fulfilled the promise: "Thy days may be long upon the land." The family line continued. Ruth's days were lengthened by an advantageous marriage and a son who would care for her one day. Additionally, when Ruth bore Obed, her first son, the women of the town said to Naomi, "And [the Lord] shall be unto thee a restorer of thy life, and a nourisher of thine old age: for thy daughter in law, which loveth thee, which is better to thee than seven sons, hath born him" (Ruth 4:15). By having a grandchild and solicitous daughter-in-law, Naomi was nourished in body and soul, and the quality of her life was extended. We read at the end of the book of Ruth that Obed is the father of Jesse, the father of David, the line through which the Messiah would come. What a royal and blessed line Ruth provided! She and Naomi would have missed these eternal, reciprocal blessings had Ruth not followed her mother-in-law.

Moses is another example how we as parents can bless our children through honoring our parents. He led the children of Israel through forty years of discipleship in the desert. In the beginning, the people were much like children—unable to solve their own problems. They looked to Moses on every matter. He complied with their endless requests and sat at judgment seat day and night. "And when Moses's father in law saw all that he did to the people, he said, What is this thing that thou doest to the people? Why sittest thou thyself alone, and all the people stand by thee from morning unto even?" (Exodus 18:14).

The Israelites would have remained in a state of immaturity under Moses's single-leadership model. He would have inhibited them to seek answers or solve their own problems. Are we likewise at fault with our children? Do we rush to solve their problems or try to do it all ourselves? Assuredly, we know more and can find solutions more efficiently and effectively than they. I sometimes hear a parent say, "I wish they would just do it my way. It would save them so much trouble!" Does it seem easier to just stand at judgment or police the fighting and arguments ourselves? Consider the long-term outcome. I firmly believe the more we allow our children to act and think for themselves and experience the consequences of their actions while they are still young, the more we foster strong, responsible children.

Jethro, Moses's father-in-law, was older and wiser in this matter. Additionally, he had an objective perspective to the predicament. Jethro told Moses what he was doing was not good. "Thou wilt surely wear away, both thou, and this people that is with thee: for this thing is too heavy for thee; thou art not able to perform it thyself alone" (Exodus 18:18). Jethro advised Moses to hearken to his voice. He counseled Moses to still represent his people before God, but that he should teach them the laws and ordinances and show them "the way wherein thy must walk, and the work that they must do" (Exodus 18:20). He told Moses to save his strength by appointing leaders to share his burden, allowing the people to grow and learn and think for themselves.

Similarly, prophets have taught us how righteous leaders allow others to exercise their agency. President Kimball remarked, "When asked how he governed so many people, the Prophet Joseph Smith said, 'I teach them correct principles, and they govern themselves.'"[1] Elder F. Enzio Busche offered this insight into self-governance:

> We try to guide our children toward self-respect and worth and mostly leave it up to them to judge themselves. We have experienced the fact that one is not as good a teacher when one discovers and points out mistakes . . . as when one helps a child discover for himself that he is doing wrong. When a child can comprehend his mistakes himself, the first step to change has already been taken. . . . I don't think there can be greater joy for parents than to see a child handle himself well in a difficult situation.[2]

My dad exercised this principle when I was growing up. He taught me correct principles in dressing modestly. Unfortunately, there were not a lot of modest choices in my small town when it came to swimwear! My choices were either racks of stylish bikinis or a few plain, utilitarian, one-piece swimwear that had all the glamour of a wetsuit. I shopped and shopped, hoping to find something attractive that also met the "modest" standard. There was nothing. My dad finally said, "You know the importance of dressing modestly. I'm sorry there aren't more choices for you, but you do what you think is right." Once he said that, the fight was over. I wore the most unattractive suit that summer to the pool where modesty was the minority. I felt it had inscribed across the front: "Hey, I'm a Mormon. I dress funny like this." The funny thing is, though, how that lesson stayed with me. I am ever-vigilant in helping my three daughters wear modest (but cute!) swimsuits. Thank goodness we have more choices now!

In a conference message, Elder David A. Bednar asked each of us:

Are you and I helping our children become agents who act and seek learning by study and by faith, or have we trained our children to wait to be taught and acted upon? Are we as parents primarily giving our children the equivalent of spiritual fish to eat, or are we consistently helping them to act, to learn for themselves, and to stand steadfast and immovable? Are we helping our children become anxiously engaged in asking, seeking, and knocking? [see 3 Nephi 14:7][3]

The commandment's blessing of a long life is realized in Moses. He would not have persisted long as the only full-time judge. He was wearing out physically and emotionally, and his life would have been shortened had he not honored the behest of Jethro. He must have lacked his own family time, rest and relaxation, and spiritual renewal. These are all necessary elements for us to be effective parents. We must learn to walk the fine line between allowing our children to "govern themselves" while also teaching general principles and offering experienced advice when necessary. Moses-like, we should not be too proud or self-involved to consider advice given by those whose experience transcends our own.

I have been "worn away" at times in parenting, doing it ineffectively. The demands of raising children are well described as a mother hen being pecked to death by her baby chicks! I've never regretted listening to the advice of my elders and changing my methods and views when necessary. I have also solicited help from others so I did not carry the load myself. Teaching my children self-governance and how to do their chores correctly has saved my energy in the long run. Fortunately for Moses, he "hearkened to the voice of his father in law, and did all that he had said" (Exodus 18:24).

We can also uncover scriptural examples of children who neglected to honor their parents. The harmful effects and destruction of families is evident. Isaac bestowed special rights and responsibilities under the Abrahamic covenant to Esau as the firstborn son of twins. Instead, Esau followed appetite more than duty to parents. Esau was famished after hunting one day and approached his brother, Jacob, with a proposition to trade his birthright for some bread and pottage of lentils. After his meal, the scriptures report, "Esau despised his birthright" (Genesis 25:34). When Esau was forty years old, he rebelled against his parents and married women that met his parents' disapproval, which brought "grief of mind to Isaac and Rebekah" (Genesis 26:35). He and his brother Jacob became the ancestors of rival nations, the Edomites and Israelites.

I witnessed the sorrowful condition of not being true to parents on my mission in Bolivia. My companion and I had the privilege of teaching a very poor, infirm, and aged woman. Her daughter and her family lived quite comfortably in a spacious house next to her, but she was separated from them. They relegated her to a small converted storage room in the back of the courtyard. It had no plumbing, ventilation, lighting, windows, or basic cooking equipment. She heated water over a primitive propane burner and often singed her hair in the unpredictable, open flames. The walls were black with soot, and the room was sparsely furnished. Her children did not provide any more than this, and I never saw her invited into their house to eat with them.

My companion and I began a quest for better living conditions for our elderly investigator. First, we acquired better cooking equipment. Next, we organized a missionary service day to scrub her sooty walls, hang up LDS posters, and wash her clothes and hair. Finally, we asked an elder with electrical skills to connect the hanging wires to a new socket so we could insert a bulb to hang from the ceiling of her room. This experience was symbolic to her conversion: "The people that walked in darkness have seen a great light: they that dwell in the land of the shadow of death, upon them had the light shined" (Isaiah 9:2). Even though her daughter professed to be a member of the Church, she did not attend on Sundays nor come to her mother's baptism. We heard later she cut the wires and removed the bulb. She explained they didn't want to pay for extra electricity.

It's interesting that with both Ruth and Moses, it was their in-laws to whom they were so loyal. We read that the lives of Ruth and Moses were literally preserved so they could raise their children. They honored and lived. Additionally, that blessing can also come full circle. We can extend the blessing of intergenerational caregiving to our families. As we lovingly care for our elderly parents and allow our children to see our example and participate in honoring, serving, and respecting them to the end of their lives, we establish a pattern to follow.

My children are the beneficiaries of observing their grandparents and participating in the caregiving of their great-grandparents. My in-laws lived close to my mother-in-law's parents and spent many years overseeing their care. My mother- and father-in-law finally moved her aging parents into their own home to lovingly offer continual care. My in-laws gave incredible instrumental and emotional support during the declining years. Three years later after moving them in, her father passed away at age 99 and her mother passed away at age 103 after living with them for ten years. I have no doubt that the quality and length of their final years were extended because of the exemplary care they received by their adult daughter and son-in-law. These were the most tender, relevant lessons any of us could learn on what it means to honor and respect one's parents.

Elder Boyd K. Packer shared a similar family legacy:

> My wife and I have seen our grandparents and then our parents leave us. Some experiences that we first thought to be burdens or trouble have long since been reclassified as blessings.
>
> My wife's father died in our home. He needed constant care. Nurses taught our children how to care for our bedridden grandpa. What they learned is of great worth to them and to us. How grateful we are to have had him close to us.
>
> We were repaid a thousand times over by the influence he had on our children. That was a great experience for our children, one I learned as a boy when Grandpa Packer died in our home.[4]

Circumstances may not allow us to directly care for our aging parents, but we can be similarly wise and compassionate stewards over their comfort and care. President Gordon B. Hinckley reflected: "I am so profoundly grateful for the love and solicitude of our children toward their mother and their father. How beautiful is the picture of a son or daughter going out of his or her way to assist with kindness and benevolence and love an aged parent."[5] As we age ourselves, we hope our children will continue that legacy with us. We can all relate to the bumper sticker that reads: "Be nice to your children. They will pick your nursing home." If we have raised children with compassion, we will likely experience compassion at their hands. There is strong correlation to honoring parents and a better quality of life in our advancing years so our days may be long and rich upon the earth.

All through the scriptures we can find examples like Ruth and Moses who kept the fourth commandment and honored their parents. Jesus taught this last loving lesson from the cross. His duty, as eldest son in the family, was to care for his mother. But that would be impossible with his premature death. He suffered great agony during the crucifixion, yet he observed his grieving and destitute mother standing near John. He said, "Woman behold thy son" and then turned to his beloved Apostle and entreated, "Behold thy mother!" (John 19:26–27). He entrusted these two to each other's care. They were to be mother and son from that day forward.

As Jesus was completing the final hour of the infinite Atonement for you and for me, I find it incredibly moving that he openly taught us all to care for our aging parents. He could have made these arrangements with Mary and John quietly and privately ahead of time. It was a very personal family matter. Yet he publicly announced to all from the cross that honoring our father and mother is a supreme godlike trait. Once Christ had seen to it that John accepted to care for Mary in this tender scene, notice what John records next: "After this, Jesus knowing that *all things were now accomplished* . . ." (John 19:28; italics added). His life's mission, with all the miraculous healings, splendid acts of mercy, and divine teachings, and His infinite Atonement, was not complete until he completely honored his mother. John records that from that time onward, he took Mary to his home to care for her.

Parenting principles from Ruth and Moses: In honoring our parents, we teach our children the attitudes and behaviors we want them to have toward their elders. Childrearing is a daunting task, so it is requisite to look to those with more experience and wisdom and consider their advice. We preserve ourselves by teaching our children correct principles and self-governance so they develop strength and independence in solving problems and making mature decisions. Christ taught that honoring parents is one of the crowning achievements of this life.

NOTES

1. Spencer W. Kimball, "Fundamental Principles to Ponder and Live," *Ensign,* November 1978, 45.

2. F. Enzio Busche, "Provoke Not Your Children," *Ensign,* March 1976, 42.

3. David A. Bednar, "Watching with All Perseverance," *Ensign,* May 2010, 43.

4. Boyd K. Packer, "The Golden Years," *Ensign,* May 2003, 83–84.

5. Gordon B. Hinckley, "Personal Worthiness to Exercise the Priesthood," *Ensign,* May 2002, 54.

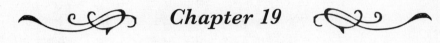

Chapter 19

THE WIDOW OF ZAREPHATH: THE POWER OF OBEYING PROPHETS

King Ahab, ruler over Israel, reigned during a period of intense wickedness during 874–853 B.C. In response, Elijah the prophet cursed the land with a famine to humble the people into repentance. To survive these lean years, he lived by a brook and was nourished with bread and meat brought on wings of ravens. When the brook dried up, he was commanded to enter the city of Zarephath and find a certain widow there. We never learn her name, yet she is one of the most esteemed women in scripture.

The famine had depleted the people of Zarephath. Elijah found the beleaguered woman gathering sticks and asked for a vessel to draw water and a morsel of bread. She replied, "As the Lord thy God liveth, I have not a cake, but an handful of meal in the barrel, and a little oil in a cruse: and, behold, I am gathering two sticks, that I may go in and dress it for me and my son, that we may eat it, and die" (1 Kings 17:12). The widow was undoubtedly in the most indigent condition, bereft of hope and near death. Yet this prophet gave her a trial by faith: "Fear not; go and do as thou hast said: but make me thereof a little cake first, and bring it unto me, and after make for thee and for thy son" (1 Kings 17:13).

It is astonishing to ask a dying mother to release her last morsel of bread to a stranger and then to have enough faith that God would provide. His careful instructions are insightful in this fragile situation. He could have allowed her to eat first and then produce the miracle for himself. But that was not the purpose of this meeting. He promises her if she did this deed, her "barrel of meal shall not waste, neither shall the cruse of oil fail, until the day that the Lord sendeth rain upon the earth" (1 Kings 17:14). This typifies the promise given by Moroni: "I would show unto the world that faith is things which are hoped for and not seen; wherefore, dispute not because ye see not, for ye receive no witness until after the trial of your faith" (Ether 12:6).

The widow's story cannot be read without personal examination. To what lengths would we go to save our child's life? Would we have given up our last handful of food believing our child would be saved through miraculous intervention? Would we relinquish it to feed a stranger? The scriptures do not reveal if she knew he was a prophet at this time, but she must have sensed his prophetic promise and obeyed. I imagine a steady hand as she poured out the last drops of oil and fried the last patty of flour to offer Elijah. She gave all she had to the prophet. What must she have thought as she watched him eat her son's last meal? The promised miracle was immediate. Her stores of food never emptied even though she did not replenish them, and she, her son, and her household had many meals thereafter.

The widow of Zarephath is a brief yet formative figure of faith, obedience, and sacrifice. She chose to follow the prophet first, even as her life and her son's life were in jeopardy. As a result, Elijah saved her son not once, but twice. At a later period, her son fell gravely ill to the point of death, and she cried in despair to Elijah. The prophet restored his life in yet another merciful miracle. She asserted, "Now by this I know that thou art a man of God, and that the word of the Lord in thy mouth is truth" (1 Kings 17:24). Her story is an instructive example of righteous parenting. If we put the Lord first, and his prophet, "all these things shall be added unto [us]" (Matthew 6:33). *We must give all our will to God and His chosen servant in order to save our families.*

Perhaps a lesser-known woman in the Old Testament was noted as a "great woman" (2 Kings 4:8). She was also never named, but was called the "Shunammite" by the prophet Elisha. This woman of Shunem undoubtedly followed the Spirit, who told her it was a man of God who passed her home so frequently. She was not given a severe trial like the woman of Zarephath, but she voluntarily gave from what she had under better circumstances. The Shunammite convinced her husband to fix a room in their house and offered food and lodging to Elisha and his servant. The prophet was so grateful for her charity that he asked what he could do to bless her. Finding her barren, and her husband old, he blessed her with a child within a year. The blessing came as promised (see 2 Kings 4:9–17).

We are given a second witness from this mother of Shunem that honoring the Lord's chosen servant blesses families. Her son grew and went to visit his father in the fields one day. Suddenly, the lad suffered a head trauma and died. The Shunammite, a great woman of faith and action, saddled an ass and rode urgently to Mount Carmel, where the prophet abode. It was a fifteen-mile journey, but she believed Elisha to be a man of God who could any perform miracle, even raising the dead. Despite the long journey on a slow animal and Elisha's delayed arrival, she had faith in the prophet. He brought the boy back to life, and mother and son were reunited (see 2 Kings 4:18–37).

Consistent with the widow of Zarephath and the Shunammite woman, honoring the prophet can save our children in temporal ways, but fundamentally, it is for our family's spiritual salvation that we heed and follow him. Elder Kevin R. Duncan said, "Trusting in and following the prophets is more than a blessing and a privilege. President Ezra Taft Benson declared that 'our [very] salvation hangs on' following the prophet."[1] We learn from the account of Elisha, the prophet at the time of Naaman, that following the prophet often does not require us to "do some great thing" (2 Kings 5:13) but usually tries our simple faith and obedience. Elder Jeffrey R. Holland reminded us, "I know we can each do something, however small that act may seem to be. We can pay an honest tithe and give our fast and free-will offerings, according to our circumstances. . . . We can share the loaves we have and trust God that the cruse of oil will not fail."[2]

The words of living prophets are modern scripture to us and words from God. "What I the Lord have spoken, I have spoken, and I excuse not myself; and though the heavens and the earth pass away, my word shall not pass away, but shall all be fulfilled, whether by mine own voice or by the voice of my servants, it is the same" (D&C 1:38). By following his counsel, the prophet will guide us through these perilous and glorious times of the latter-day dispensation. Elder Claudio R. M. Costa testified, "It is a great blessing to receive the word, commandments, and guidance of the Lord in these difficult days of the earth. The prophet can be inspired to see the future in benefit of mankind."[3]

President Gordon B. Hinckley, called as a prophet of God, saw the future accountability of family members:

> I am confident that when we stand before the bar of God, there will be little mention of how much wealth we accumulated in life or of any honors which we may have achieved. But there will be searching questions concerning our domestic relations. And I am convinced that only those who have walked through life with love and respect and appreciation for their companions and children will receive from our eternal judge the words, "Well done, thou good and faithful servant: . . . enter thou into the joy of thy lord" [Matthew 25:21].[4]

Prophets see into the future and are thus named "seers." Another word for "seer" is "watchman." Watchmen were placed on the top of Nephite towers to scout for enemies. Who are these watchmen today? Certainly parents with stewardship over their families, but also our prophets. They can "see" what is coming to all nations and the enemy as he advances. He has the position of perspective and keys to lead and guide the Lord's kingdom in safety. Elder Quentin L. Cook shared this example:

> Sometimes prophets teach us prophetic priorities that provide protection for us now and in the future. As an example, President David O. McKay was the prophet from 1951 to 1970. One area of significant focus was his emphasis on the family. He taught that no success in life can compensate for failure in the home. He encouraged members to strengthen families by increasing religious observance. His teachings were a protection from the disintegration of the institution of marriage that came after his death. Because of President McKay's teaching, the Latter-day Saints strengthened their commitment to family and eternal marriage.[5]

I witness that prophets are called of God. They manifest His voice and His love and His counsel to us as we walk forth courageously to raise families. My father-in-law gave the following account at my son's Eagle Scout court of honor. It beautifully illustrates the need to follow the guides put here on earth to lead us to safety.

> Dar Reese was an outstanding professor of chemistry at Oregon State University, but more than that, he was a great outdoorsman and one of the most respected scouters in the area. He also was a consultant for

Coleman camping equipment. He worked for the forest service and helped plan and lay out the Pacific Crest Trail.

I was lucky enough to have backpacked with Dar a few times and was with him on his last fifty-mile hike on the Pacific Crest Trail with a group of Scouts and leaders he had invited. He planned everything in detail. We started at a point where we could hike north. He insisted that we be on the trail by 7:00 a.m. so we would always have the sun at our backs. We would also be into a campground by a good lake for swimming and fishing before the heat of the day. He even showed us where to walk when we were climbing or going downhill.

As we would hike down the trail, he was constantly teaching. When we would have a rest stop, he would advise us according to what lay ahead. "This stretch has plenty of water, so there is no need to carry much with you." Or, "There is no water ahead for about five miles, so make sure your canteens are full." As we were hiking along he would encourage us with something like, "Just around this next bend there is a nice little lake that has a cool meadow. That will be a good place to stop for lunch."

There were sometimes steep and rocky places on the trail and sometimes the backpacks got heavy, but it was a great and enjoyable fifty-miler. As we finished the hike, everybody remarked about what a great time we had enjoyed and when we could do it again.

While we were waiting at the end of the trail for our transportation home, another Scout troop came dragging in. They had hiked down from the north. They had the sun beating in their faces almost the whole way. They had arrived at their first planned camp and found the stream had dried up and there was no water. They hiked another twelve miles to find a campsite. They were beat and unhappy and didn't want to ever go on another fifty-miler.

What a difference it makes to follow someone who has been down the trail. Someone who knows where the cool and shady places of respite are. Someone to show us how to do things at the proper time so we can avoid the heat of the day when it is not necessary. How to prepare for the things that lie ahead.

That is what good Scoutmasters do. But there are many others that know the trail. If we are wise, we will look to those that know and follow their counsel. Parents, grandparents, experienced leaders, and others can help you enjoy the trek down the trail. Follow Church leaders, especially the prophet and General Authorities. I guarantee they have been down the trail and know the rough spots and where the places of refuge are and how to prepare for what lies ahead.

Most important, follow the Savior. He is the ultimate guide. If we do, although there may be some steep and rocky places on the trail, when we get to the end here on earth, we will look back and say, "That was a good hike. I am glad I was able to come. I would do that again."

Parenting principles from the widow of Zarephath: Follow the prophet and his counsel and all things will work for our good. Prophets are the "seers" of our day who stand at the watchtower and warn us of the enemy. We need to give our all to the Lord and obey His chosen servants.

NOTES

1.   Kevin R. Duncan, "Our Very Survival," *Ensign,* November 2010, 35.

2.   Jeffrey R. Holland, "A Handful of Meal and a Little Oil," *Ensign,* May 1996, 31.

3.   Claudio R. M. Costa, "Obedience to the Prophets," *Ensign,* November 2010, 11.

4.   Gordon B. Hinckley, "Personal Worthiness to Exercise the Priesthood," *Ensign,* May 2002, 54.

5.   Quentin L. Cook, "Give Heed unto the Prophets' Words," *Ensign,* May 2008, 48–49.

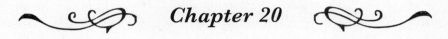

Chapter 20

GOD AND MOSES: THE POWER
OF INDIVIDUAL WORTH

In the evolution of parenting, we ultimately raise our children to leave us one day (although some children are more anxious to leave our "nest" than others!). Our earnest desire is for them to become steadfast and sure sons and daughters of God who will one day form their own family unions and be righteous parents themselves. While slowly relinquishing control, we need to affirm to our children that they are of worth and can always receive guidance through a divine relationship with their Heavenly Father. Then, when we are no longer able to maintain direct influence, they can rely on an inseparable tie to their Heavenly Parent. We only have a few short years to do that great work.

The three great pillars of doctrine in the restored gospel are the Creation, the Fall, and the Atonement. If our children learn, understand, and believe these fundamental principles, they will be on sure footing as they strike out on their own. We examine here the doctrine of the Creation and how God esteems His children above all His creations. In Moses chapter 1, God revealed in vision the immensity of His creations:

> And it came to pass, as the voice was still speaking, Moses cast his eyes and beheld the earth, yea, even all of it; and there was not a particle of it which he did not behold, discerning it by the Spirit of God.
>
> And he beheld also the inhabitants thereof, and there was not a soul which he beheld not; and he discerned them by the Spirit of God;

and their numbers were great, even numberless as the sand upon the sea shore.

And he beheld many lands; and each land was called earth, and there were inhabitants on the face thereof. (vv. 27–29)

Moses was no doubt overcome with his nothingness after his eyes were opened to comprehend all living things. He asked God how all things came into being and how God created every particle he beheld (see Moses 1:30). Our omnipotent Heavenly Father offered Moses only a brief answer. It was not requisite Moses be instructed with details he was not capable of understanding. Summarizing verses 31–35, God told Moses that through His Son was the earth made, that His workmanship was for His own purposes, and He was wise not to tell Moses how or why everything was made. In fact, Heavenly Father reminded Moses that He was limiting His instruction to the planet Moses dwelled upon and did not include the numberless worlds also created by Him. In other words, "It is enough for you to know that I have numbered them and they are *mine*."

The God and Moses account is a reminder to us that there are many things we do not understand. It remains in God's wisdom *not* to reveal all things to us. It's like a four-year-old who asks what makes a car run. I could say, "Gas," but that is a simplified, incomplete answer. Yet that sliver of information would be enough for most children that age. In withholding answers, Heavenly Father also wants us to exercise our faith that He is in charge. He numbers His children; they are known to Him, and we need to be faithful even when we don't know how or why.

With that background, it is stunning that immediately after this exchange between Moses and God, we learn we are His crowning achievement and we can become like Him one day. During the seven periods of creation, man and woman were the last and greatest of all God's creations. At the end of the sixth day, He surveyed all His creations and called them "good" (see Moses 2:31). It wasn't until His children were created that He used that word. Elder Dieter F. Uchtdorf marveled, "In other words, the vast expanse of eternity, the glories and mysteries of infinite space and time are all built for the benefit of ordinary mortals like you and me. Our Heavenly Father created the universe that we might reach our potential as His sons and daughters. This is the paradox of man: compared to God, man is nothing; yet we are everything to God."[1]

Of all the titles that God possesses, He chose for us to call Him "Father," signifying our personal and lasting relationship to Him. He continues to work for and glory in the salvation of His children (see Moses 1:39). An insightful exercise is to count how often God tenderly called Moses "my son" in Moses 1:1–7. On one hand, God swept his arm over all His numberless creations while his other arm encircled Moses, His son. We see something of our loving Father's priorities and how our parenting priorities need to be checked as well. Our other "creations" (work, community and church service, hobbies, friends, and other worthwhile pursuits) should not overshadow a single child. Do we emphasize our stewardship over a child as "our son" or "our daughter"? No other earthly accomplishment matters in comparison. No other creation can be called as "good." I am reminded that a man on his deathbed never laments, "I wish I had spent more time at the office."

Furthermore, God told Moses he was of such worth because he was made in the similitude of His Only Begotten (see Moses 1:6). In what ways is that true? First, they were both created in the physical image of God, as were we. Next, the etymology of Moses's name suggests "son" in Egyptian and "to deliver" in Hebrew—the description of Christ. Additionally, Moses and Jesus lived under parallel circumstances: when they were both infants, a jealous king decreed that all children be killed and both parents were forced to hide their sons; they were sent to be deliverers—Moses freed the children of Israel from temporal bondage (slavery under the Egyptians) and Christ gave us freedom from both physical (death) and spiritual (sin) bondage; and both gave the law to the children of Israel. Moses lifted the serpent on the pole to save the Israelites just as Jesus was lifted on the cross to save us.

In what ways are we created in similitude of Christ? We are creators when we take upon ourselves the sacred powers of procreation. The word itself declares we are for ("pro") creation. We are saviors when we engage in the redemptive work in temples for the deceased. We are partakers of His mercies when we forgive another. We can receive all the Father hath and be glorified with Him through the Atonement of our Redeemer, as joint-heirs with Christ. In Romans 8:15–17, we read: "For ye have not received the spirit of bondage again to fear; but ye have received the Spirit of adoption, whereby we cry, Abba, Father. The Spirit itself beareth witness with our spirit, that we are the children of God: And if children, then heirs; heirs of God, and joint-heirs with Christ; if so be that we suffer with him, that we may be also glorified together." Do our children know their relationship to Christ and our Eternal Father in Heaven? Do they know how transcendent and sublime it is to be a part of the plan of exaltation? If our children could just understand and remember these principles, it would seem impossible to ever stray from the right.

Such was the case with Moses. After he understood the love God had for him and his relationship as a son, Satan came to tempt him. He offered Moses distractions from the eternal truths he had just received. He represented the vainglories of the world and asserted, "Moses, son of man, worship me" (Moses 1:12). Satan contorted the eternal relationship into a cheapened version by calling him "son of man." He did not recognize or value the divine within Moses as *God's son*.

Moses was not fooled. He had just stood before the Light of the World, the Eternal Father, who esteemed his worth considering the immensities of heaven. Moses saw the contrast between real and false, between light and darkness. He responded to Satan in one of the most powerful confrontations in all scripture: "Who art thou? For behold, I am a son of God, in the similitude of his Only Begotten; and where is thy glory, that I should worship thee? . . . Blessed be the name of my God, for his Spirit hath not altogether withdrawn from me, or else where is thy glory, for it is darkness unto me? And I can judge between thee and God; for God said unto me: Worship God, for him only shalt thou serve. Get thee hence, Satan; deceive me not; for God said unto me: Thou art after the similitude of mine Only Begotten" (Moses 1:13, 15–16). Endowed by power, Moses scorned Satan and reaffirmed his worth. He could easily discern, or judge, between the temporary temptations of Satan and the eternal rewards of God. The same can be true if our children are taught and hold fast to principles from on high.

We all have worth! We all matter to God! These should be beliefs firmly rooted in our children's hearts and minds. When I look at my beautiful children in tender moments, I try to tell them, "Heavenly Father must love me so much to have chosen you to be my child." If children feel loved by their parents who they *can* see, it will be easier for them to imagine a loving Heavenly Father who they *can't* see. We are the embodiment of heavenly parenting on earth. Those whose only experience with parents has been harsh, chaotic, and unloving could find difficulty seeing God as otherwise. Moreover, for those who abuse children, Christ gave this warning: "It were better for him that a millstone were hanged about his neck, and he cast into the sea, than that he should offend one of these little ones" (Luke 17:2).

A tangible way to hold on to the truths of a loving God is when our youth receive and review their patriarchal blessings. Like Jeremiah, they will discover that God knew them before birth (see Jeremiah 1:4–5). Like Esther, they will realize they have been sent to earth for "such a time as this" (Esther 4:14). "I am a child of God" should not just be a line we sing, but a truth we live by. When my eldest son was a teenager, I printed off a quote by President Ezra Taft Benson, framed it, and hung it above his bed until he left home:

> We have great confidence in you. You are not just ordinary young men and young women. You are choice spirits, many of you having been held back in reserve for almost 6,000 years to come forth in this day, at this time, when the temptations, responsibilities, and opportunities are the very greatest.
>
> God loves you as He loves each and every one of His children, and His desire and purpose and glory is to have you return to Him pure and undefiled, having proven yourselves worthy of an eternity of joy in His presence.[2]

There are many families who rehearse this declaration (or something similar) to their children: "Remember who you are and what you stand for." My neighbor repeated that phrase every time her children left the house. Years later, when her youngest was in college, she found herself single and beginning to date again. One day, she went on a hike with her then future-husband. They ended up cresting the peak of Rock Canyon where many college students drive to park. As they walked by cars with amorous couples inside, she was surprised to see her college son with his friends. Even more awkward was his realization that his middle-aged mother was with her boyfriend in the same place where *he* was hanging out. Soon after, he drove past his mom and yelled out the window, "Hey, Mom! Remember who you are and what you stand for!"

In speaking of individual worth, the teachings of Christ from the New Testament are invaluable, such as the parable of the talents. This parable affirms that talents and gifts are given to each of God's children to exercise and develop on earth. To some are given one talent, to others, two talents, and to others are given five talents. "Talents" evoke the metaphor of gifts with which we are endowed, not just the literal meaning of money in this parable.

The master gave each of these three servants talents "according to his several ability" (Matthew 25:15). This is a reassuring, insightful phrase.

Each man was different in need, opportunity, and ability. No matter. In this parable, Christ taught that one servant was not elevated above another. They were given what was necessary and so are we, according to our several circumstances.

What stands out is the reaction of the master when his servants reported back the results of their investments. The servants who had two and five talents used them to multiply their initial investment, or in other words, they developed their God-given talents. The man who began with two talents ended up with four; the man with five returned with ten talents. To both these men, the master replied with the same praise: "Well done, thou good and faithful servant: thou hast been faithful over a few things, I will make thee ruler over many things: enter thou into the joy of thy Lord" (see verses 21 and 23). There was no need for the two-talent person to feel inadequate that he was unable to achieve ten talents like the other. He was just as important in the eyes of the master and received the same reward.

The servant who began with one talent hid it out of fear. This can be a warning to all who compare our supposed inadequacies and feel lacking. The master chastised that man, and through him, we gain instruction. We are expected to multiply our gifts, no matter the number. To each is given special abilities whose genesis is found in the pre-earth life. We are to continue identifying and developing them under the approbation of a loving Father in Heaven to build His kingdom.

From Doctrine and Covenants 46:11–12, we are given this counsel: "For all have not every gift given unto them; for there are many gifts, and to every man is given a gift by the Spirit of God. To some is given one, and to some is given another, that all may be profited thereby." This scripture reminds me that as we develop and share our instruments of ability, we are like members in an orchestra, playing a viola, French horn, or piccolo in perfect union. Some have an instrument that requires a major score to play at one time or another. Nevertheless, the audience profits thereby as they hear the symphony's exquisite music that combines each member's part at the appropriate time. Accordingly, parents are wise not to compare their children's talents with others or value one over another.

Elder L. Tom Perry offered additional insights to guide our children in developing their talents:

> Every one of our Father in Heaven's children is great in His sight. If the Lord sees greatness in you, how then should you see yourself? We

have all been blessed with many talents and abilities. Some have been blessed with the talent to sing, some to paint, some to speak, some to dance, some to create beautiful things with their hands, and others to render compassionate service. Some may possess many, others only a few. It matters not the size or the quantity but the effort we put forth to develop the talents and abilities we have received. You are not competing with anyone else. You are only competing with yourself to do the best with whatever you have received. Each talent that is developed will be greatly needed and will give you tremendous fulfillment and satisfaction during your life.[3]

The parable of the talents also reflects the gifts of parenting. We learn we have differing abilities as stewards over God's children. Parents are each unique and raise their family depending on how they were raised, on their circumstances, personalities, opportunities, and desires. A righteous parent does not lament what he or she lacks, nor does he or she compare talents with others. Instead, he increases the good gifts he has been given and uses his agency to bless his family. Latter-day Saints have the gifts of the gospel, the scriptures, prophets and apostles, and personal revelation to instruct and support them in their duty as parents. Each of these can help us magnify our several abilities. There has never been a more enlightened dispensation in the earth's history, and the Lord has said, "Of him unto whom much is given much is required" (D&C 82:3). If we magnify our calling as parents and stay true to our covenants, we will be rewarded with infinite posterity and dominion. We will be welcomed with that same reward: "Well done, thou good and faithful servant: thou hast been faithful over a few things, I will make thee ruler over many things: enter thou into the joy of thy Lord" (Matthew 25:21).

We learn self-worth from the father-son relationship between God and Moses in the Pearl of Great Price. To our Father, we are His beloved sons and daughters, and He knows us by name. The adversary wants to demean that esteem and have us think we are just temporal beings. We are not. We are spiritual beings, gods in embryo, on an earthly journey toward exaltation. Think of the power these truths contain as our children make crucial decisions throughout their lives.

Parenting principles from God and Moses: We each have been given special talents to exercise and increase as wise stewards in families. Our children need to appreciate their estimable value from the Supreme Creator. They need to believe in and act as the literal spirit sons and daughters of God. If we can help them gain a testimony of their singular worth, when they leave our homes, these precious principles will help ground them firmly in righteous living.

NOTES

1. Dieter F. Uchtdorf, "You Matter to Him," *Ensign,* November 2011, 20.

2. Ezra Taft Benson, "A Message to the Rising Generation," *Ensign,* November 1977, 30.

3. L. Tom Perry, "Youth of the Noble Birthright," *Ensign,* November 1998, 74.

Conclusion

How blessed we are to have the perfect parenting manual—the scriptures! While you read this book, did you see mothers and fathers within the standard works as real people with daily worries, like you, doing their best to raise children in truth and light? Did you identify with any of their struggles? Did their undaunted faith inspire you to persevere with hope? Elder Richard G. Scott witnessed,

> Throughout the ages, Father in Heaven has inspired select men and women to find, through the guidance of the Holy Ghost, solutions to life's most perplexing problems. He has inspired those authorized servants to record those solutions as a type of handbook for those of His children who have faith in His plan of happiness and in His Beloved Son, Jesus Christ. We have ready access to this guidance through the treasure we call the standard works—that is, the Old and New Testaments, the Book of Mormon, the Doctrine and Covenants, and the Pearl of Great Price.[1]

Perhaps this is the first time you have read these passages with a parenting perspective. That is the beauty and infinite wealth of the scriptures—each time we study with a different focus, we elevate our understanding. It is like putting on new glasses and seeing something in detail for the first time. What were the insights you gained while reading certain chapters? What principles addressed your most immediate concerns? Did you write down the strokes of ideas you received? Will you act on them? The discussion questions following this concluding chapter will help you make goals and follow through with your commitments in your sacred stewardship as a parent. Invite the Holy Ghost, who is the bearer of all truth, to strengthen you in your righteous desires. Make scripture study, prayer, and personal reflection a daily part of your parenting practice. Go to the temple to create a blueprint for raising each child.

We can and *should* make daily changes. Elder David A. Bednar spoke of the power of the scriptures: "The Book of Mormon is our handbook of instructions as we travel the pathway from bad to good to better and strive to have our hearts changed."[2] For all who struggle to improve their parenting, the power of the Atonement of Christ is the way up and way out of poor behaviors and self-defeating thoughts. The Atonement is not only available for cleansing us from sin, but also for enabling us to purify our lives. Elder Bednar elaborated,

> The Atonement provides help for us to overcome and avoid bad and to do and become good. Help from the Savior is available for the entire journey of mortality—from bad to good to better and to change our very nature. . . .
>
> The Savior has suffered not just for our iniquities but also for the inequality, the unfairness, the pain, the anguish, and the emotional distresses that so frequently beset us. . . . The Son of God perfectly knows and understands, for He felt and bore our burdens before we ever did. And because He paid the ultimate price and bore that burden, He has perfect empathy and can extend to us His arm of mercy in so many phases of our life. He can reach out, touch, succor—literally run to us—and strengthen us to be more than we could ever be and help us to do that which we could never do through relying only upon our own power.[3]

Finally, the Atonement enables us to bear our burdens with joy. That may not seem a reality when family trials are so troubling and seemingly endless. In spite of these, we can look to Alma and the newly converted Nephites as examples of patience and peace in suffering. They were obedient and faithful, yet found themselves in bondage to the Lamanites (see Mosiah chapter 24). Like Alma and his followers, parents may be doing their best. Yet parents today find themselves raising challenging children through no fault of their own. And like the Nephites in bondage, we can pour out our hearts to heaven and access the marvelous power of Christ's Atonement. The people of Alma found the Lord heard their prayers, and their burdens were "made light; yea, the Lord did strengthen them that they could bear up their burdens with ease, and they did submit cheerfully and with patience to the will of the Lord" (Mosiah 24:15). With joy.

Parenting *is* a joyful journey. I testify of that. The plan of salvation allows men and women to come to earth "that they might have joy" in families (2 Nephi 2:25). We have been organized into the perfect eternal unit to practice godlike attributes and better ourselves. In families, we are reminded daily of our commitment to move forward on the iron rod and find the tree of life together. Our Heavenly Father has graciously given us His spirit children for us to lead and guide down the straight and narrow path. Often, it is the little child who does the teaching. We are humbled by their ability to quickly forgive; our hearts are softened by their tender feelings; we feel more determined to become more like them: "submissive, meek, humble, patient, full of love, willing to submit to all things which the Lord seeth fit to inflict upon him, even as a child doth submit to his father" (Mosiah 3:19). If we yield to the powerful principles found in the word of God, we can be found on the right hand of God in glory and exaltation, together with our loved ones, forever.

NOTES

1.   Richard G. Scott, "The Power of Scripture," *Ensign*, November 2011, 6.

2.   David A. Bednar, "The Atonement and the Journey of Mortality," *Ensign*, April 2012, 40.

3.   Bednar, "The Atonement and the Journey of Mortality," 42, 47.

 # Discussion Questions

The following can be used for individual reflection, or for couple or group book discussion. Remember the counsel in Mosiah 4:27:

> And see that all these things are done in wisdom and order; for it is not requisite that a man should run faster than he has strength. And again, it is expedient that he should be diligent, that thereby he might win the prize; therefore, all things must be done in order.

These exercises are meant to be encouraging, not discouraging. Therefore, be prayerful and careful about which parenting principles you would like to work on. Do not do more at a time than you are able, but do them in "wisdom and order." We are not required to be perfect in all things in mortality, but to be diligently working on what we can improve on.

1. During a normal parent-child interaction period (getting ready for school in the morning, eating dinner together, doing Saturday chores, etc.), how many positive to negative statements do you find yourself saying? Make a conscious effort to count. Consider recording yourself for accuracy. Are you saying at least eight positive statements to one negative statement? If not, this would be a good area to make a goal for improvement. See chapter 1.

2. Think of a typical parent-child disagreement in your family. Which child is most likely to turn that situation into a power struggle? How could you reframe the request to include more options rather than giving one direct order? In other words, are you giving more choices they *can* do than *can't* within acceptable boundaries? See chapter 1.

3. Do you find yourself in stressful situations making empty threats, or consequences, to your child(ren) that you don't uphold? Write some of these down and why they failed. Review chapter 1 and work on making more reasonable consequences tied to expected behavior that you are able to follow through with. Invite your child(ren) to help define what would be some reasonable consequences you both can agree on.

4. When your child is communicating something important, how is your body language? Do your facial expressions and posture invite intimacy and trust? Do you maintain eye contact whenever possible and give them undivided attention? If not, what is dividing your attention? How can you balance the child's needs with other demands or remove competing distractions?

5. Review a recent struggle your child had. In what ways did you validate or invalidate their feelings? Write down some of the things you said in response to their emotions. Is there any way you could improve, using more empathetic listening and validating than harsh judging and criticism? See chapter 1.

6. Review chapters 1, 2, 9, 12, 17, and 18 and list attributes of Christ as he ministered to others. In which of these attributes do you find yourself desiring to improve? Pick one and make a goal to emulate the Savior more in your life.

7. Read Mosiah 29 and list the characteristics of a government where the citizens are given agency. How does this empower the people to grow in maturity? How is your family structure and parenting style similar or dissimilar to that of Mosiah's? Also review Lehi's example in chapter 3 and what Moses learned from his father-in-law in chapter 18 as the best leadership model. How are you allowing your child(ren) to exercise agency and learn from their successes and mistakes?

8. Think of the last sibling quarrel you witnessed. Did you focus more on the desired outcome rather than the undesirable behavior? Do you emphasize the positive in children when redirecting behavior? Do you emphasize the "being" rather than the "doing" and teach doctrine? See chapter 2.

9. Do you find yourself stretched as a parent, meeting everyone else's needs with little leftover for yourself? Consider the tree of life account of Lehi being nourished by the tree as he leads his family toward salvation in 1 Nephi 8. How can you taste of the love of God on a daily basis in order to offer it more bountifully to others? Commit to small but significant ways you can begin nourishing yourself better so you can stand with love and power to those you minister to. See chapter 3.

10. What worldly choices are crowding your time? How many daily minutes are spent one-on-one with your child(ren)? Make a log of actual quality time and determine total quantity per day. Are you happy with the amount? How does it compare to other *good* things such as your daily amount of entertainment? Are there any superfluous activities you should remove in order to make time for the *best* . . . your child? See chapter 4.

11. Do you tend to avoid correcting your child(ren) in serious matters? Do you shy away due to personal inadequacies, fear, or wanting to be liked or to avoid conflict? What can you learn from Alma the Younger's approach with his son Corianton in Alma 39? How can Paul's declaration in Philippians 4:13 give you strength and confidence? Read Doctrine and Covenants 121:41–44 and follow this excellent guideline, remembering that love must be already present in the parent-child relationship in order to show an increase afterward. Role play a few corrective scenarios as you practice this skill using the "sandwich" approach. See chapter 5.

12. Does your child(ren) have regular opportunities to work, sacrifice, and serve others? When was the last time? Practice using Alma the Younger's approach with his son Shiblon by inviting them with an opportunity, showing them how to do it by example, using encouragement, and praising them for their efforts. See chapter 6.

13. Is there a trait in your child that you tend to look at as a deficit? Remember the brother of Jared taking rough stones and working them into glass? How can you take the rough edges off your child and buff them smooth? One way is by looking at that trait in a positive way. Try an exercise where you reframe a negative into a

positive. See chapter 7. Another way is by accepting where that child is and believing in their potential. See chapter 9. Create a vision of them "as if" they were developing toward the potential that is uniquely theirs.

14. Review the five-layer defense approach Moroni used in fortifying cities. See chapter 8. Name at least five strategies you use in protecting your child(ren) in your home from insidious outside forces. These should include being *aware, prepared,* and *arming* you and your child(ren) with the whole armor of God (Alma 2:12). Do you have visible banners of your faith and review and recommit to them on a regular basis? These could include "The Family: A Proclamation to the World," "The Living Christ: The Testimony of the Apostles," and the current words of our prophets in the *Ensign* magazine.

15. What are the lessons of eternal parenting we learn from Hannah? See chapter 10. Are any of these principles ones you would like to practice with greater urgency in your life? Make a goal in that area. How can those who have children exercise compassion and withhold judgment to those who are childless? By the same token, how can infertile couples be gentler on themselves and other parents? Identify something in your life for which you have not received the desired blessing. How can you practice "waiting upon the Lord" each day with greater peace and confidence?

16. Make a list of your family rituals and memorials. These may include family prayer and scripture study, weekly family home evenings, preparing and eating meals together, bedtime rituals, storytelling and family history, journals, photo albums and scrapbooks, religious art, and parent-child dates and activities together. Are there few or many daily reminders of your belief in Christ? How do you spend one-on-one time with each child to *behold* them? Additionally, do you regularly share your testimony and love to your child(ren) in natural settings? When was the last time you did? See chapters 11, 12, and 15. Look over the family home evening list of activities or the questions to ask in a parent-child interview and determine if you can add any improvements to recognizing the needs of individual children in your family.

17. Compare your reaction to disappointments and irritations with your child(ren) to Moroni's and Helaman's reaction to Pahoran during their extremities in war. Which military leader's manner is more like yours? Do you internalize the words, "It mattereth not" or rise to anger too often? How often is a negative spirit taking over your home and holding hostage your relationship with your child(ren), building resentment between you? If this is an area of concern, read Colossians 3:21, Moroni 7:4, and D&C 108:7 and set specific goals for improvement. Remember how we do not measure up to perfection with our Heavenly Father and should be compassionate toward others so we can receive that same grace at judgment day. See chapter 13.

18. If Elder Holland believes the scripture John 14:27 is almost universally disobeyed, how can you gain more peace, not fear, in your life? Are you "found" as often as possible in the temple? Have you made it a priority to get your life in order to receive a temple recommend, seek solace there, and return often? Consider what blessings you are denying yourself if you are *not* worshiping at these sacred sanctuaries on earth. Finally, write down the four areas of proper child development (physically, spiritually, intellectually, and socially). List the ways you are conscientiously providing growth in each area for your child(ren). Are they well balanced? See chapter 14.

19. As you read the New Testament, highlight all the tangible objects Christ uses to teach spiritual matters. How do those visual aids help get the principles deep inside the hearts of the listeners? Are there any visual aids in your world that would be age-appropriate to use in teaching the gospel to your child(ren)? Brainstorm a list and try to use one. Be sure your child does not misunderstand the connection to be literal or by regarding the object more than the spiritual principle. Follow Christ's example of teaching by using more stories and parables. Teach the "whys" of the gospel through doctrine rather than focusing solely on behavior and teach in concrete, tangible terms that can be applied. Finally, try out one of the ideas listed for family scripture study found at the end of chapter 17.

20. Review the account of the widow of Zarepeth in 1 Kings 17 and consider that she *gave all she had to the prophet.* Are you withholding anything from the current prophet? When he speaks, do you listen, believe, and obey? In what ways have your blessings multiplied when you obeyed the modern-day prophets? Have you recorded them and told your child(ren) recently about those blessings?

21. Do you often teach the doctrine of the Creation, Fall, and Atonement to your child(ren)? Read Moses 1:1–7 and count how many times God calls Moses "my son." What does that mean to you? Do you grasp the significance of your relationship to Heavenly Father as His most divine and personal creation? Do your children know it? Do they understand their part in the journey along the path of eternal salvation? Do they know what God's plan is for them? What talents did you and your child(ren) develop in the pre-earth life? How are you identifying those talents and developing them? These are questions to revisit many times as your child(ren) grow and are able to comprehend their meaning.

About the Author

JULIE K. NELSON is a wife and mother of five children, raising them in Illinois and now Utah. She received a bachelor's degree in education from Brigham Young University and a master's degree from Utah State University in marriage, family and human development. Her scholarly research and creative writing have been published in journals and anthologies, and she has won numerous state and national awards for her writing. Julie has enjoyed teaching children in public and private schools and currently teaches at Utah Valley University.